THE END *of the*
NATION STATE

The Rise of Regional Economies

KENICHI OHMAE

THE FREE PRESS

New York   London   Toronto   Sydney   Tokyo   Singapore

The Free Press
A Division of Simon & Schuster Inc.
1230 Avenue of the Americas
New York, N.Y. 10020

Printed in the United States of America

printing number

1 2 3 4 5 6 7 8 9 10

Text design by Carla Bolte

Library of Congress Cataloging-in-Publication Data

Ōmae, Ken'ichi
        The end of the nation state: the rise of regional economies/ Kenichi Ohmae.
            p. cm.
        Includes bibliographical references (p.   ).
        ISBN 0-02-923341-0
        1. Trade blocs.   2. Regionalism.   3. International economic integration.   I. Title.
    HF1418.7.045   1995
        337.1—dc20   95-13613
                                                                         CIP

To my former colleagues at McKinsey,
who have been—and remain—a constant source of
inspiration and intellectual challenge

CONTENTS

PREFACE

Ever since I wrote *The Mind of the Strategist,* my professional activities have been largely devoted to helping managers and policymakers alike understand, adapt to, and leverage the primary forces shaping the global economy. Chief among these forces, in my view, are the irreversible effects of technology—in particular, modern information technology—on the structure of business processes and on the values, judgments, and preferences of citizens and consumers in all parts of the world. Indeed, so powerful are these effects that, once the genie of global information flow really gets out of the bottle—and it is certainly out of the bottle now—there can be no turning back. Against this kind of current, no traditional strategy, no familiar line of policy, and no entrenched form of organization can stand untouched or unchanged.

As a group, corporate managers have moved relatively quickly to embrace and accommodate, and even to exploit, this torrent of information. They have understood from the outset that their companies would not—and could not—remain immune to so fundamental a change in their environment. Government leaders, however, the men and women responsible for the affairs of both modern nation states and the assemblies of such states (the United Nations, for example, and the European Union and the parties to the North American Free Trade Act [NAFTA]), have had a very different reaction. Barring such catastrophes as unprecedented natural disaster, nuclear holocaust, or an ill-starred conventional war, they have, by and large, remained convinced that the entities they oversaw *would* remain pretty much unaffected.

Individual nations might, of course, do a little better or a little worse in the global marketplace. The quality of citizens' lives in one might improve a little faster or slower than in another. The industrial mix of value-creating activities might look a little different than it otherwise would have looked. But, surely, the information-led transition to a genuinely borderless economy would not call into question the relevance of nation states as meaningful units of economic activity. Nor would it call into question the ability of governments to "manage," at least in general terms, the evolving shape of that activity. Nor—at the bottom of it all—would it challenge the fundamental integrity or coherence of the nation state itself. To government leaders, that was positively unthinkable. On the maps that mattered, there were—and always would be—borders between countries. The precise line of demarcation might shift with events, but the fact that such lines existed would not. Of this, government leaders were quietly and confidently certain.

But they were wrong. The forces now at work *have* raised troubling questions about the relevance—and effectiveness—of nation states as meaningful aggregates in terms of which to think about, much less manage, economic activity. Once-powerful examples of such nation states *have* come apart at the seams. (At a conference of leading CEOs held in Stuttgart back in 1990, I predicted that the "global logic" unleashed by these forces would lead to the collapse of the Soviet Union. At the time, no one else in the room believed me.) And many of the core values supporting a world order based on discrete, independent nation states—liberal democracy as practiced in the West, for instance, and even the very notion of political sovereignty itself—*have* shown themselves in serious need of redefinition or, perhaps, replacement. Indeed, as the 21st century approaches and as what I call the four "I's"—industry, investment, individuals, and information—flow relatively unimpeded across national borders, the building-block concepts appropriate to a 19th-century, closed-country model of the world no longer hold.

Still, for perfectly understandable reasons, that model and those concepts remain in common, daily use. In some companies—and in most governments—there is a gap of more than a century between the cross-border realities of the external world and the framework of ideas and the principles used to make sense of them. This is not surprising. Old ideas, old explanations die hard. And the more obvious and matter-of-fact they seem, the harder they die. Therefore, my hope for this book is that, together with many of the things I have written in the past, it will provide managers, scholars, and government leaders with the beginnings of a new set of principles for thinking about why some regions prosper economically and others do not, and why traditional policies based on traditional principles simply cannot provide an adequate guide to the borderless world. It is my strong belief that, so long as the old principles continue to shape policy, the century-long gap between intention and result cannot be closed by better execution or implementation. Nothing can close it. The principles themselves have to change.

I would like to thank Alan Kantrow for his intellectual contribution and editorial assistance. Without his help, I would not have been able to crystallize my thinking to this level. Ms. Haruko Maruyama was instrumental in putting the manuscript in order. Bill Matassoni has shaped my aspiration—as he has for more than a decade—to draw a message for global readers from my primary immersion in the experience of companies and industries in Japan and Asia. I owe, as well, a special debt of gratitude to the leaders of Singapore, Malaysia, Hong Kong, and Taiwan, who have done so much to show the rest of us the kind of prosperity that is possible when local geographies are exposed to the global logic of the borderless economy.

My former colleagues at McKinsey & Company, to whom I dedicate this book, have been a constant source of inspiration and intellectual challenge. Without doubt, McKinsey is the most emphatically global organization I know in terms of membership, organization, and value system. I am fortunate to have been, for more than two decades, part of its efforts to help create genuinely global enterprises. We were able to practice what we preached.

As for myself, I have now retired from McKinsey to work with a group of citizens in Japan dedicated to reforming the country and its policies along the lines of the ideas presented in this book and in other writings of mine on the political and social situation in Japan.

Here, too, I hope to practice what I've preached.

For my friends and family, there is, of course, a special debt of gratitude. Without their affection and support, I would never have been able to sustain my enthusiasm for this new challenge. I'm sure they understand that what I am now trying to do is make it possible for them and, one day, their children to enjoy a high quality of life in the kind of country they deserve.

Introduction

WHERE THE BORDERS FALL IN A BORDERLESS WORLD

With the ending of the frigid Fifty Years' War between Soviet-style communism and the West's liberal democracy, some observers—Francis Fukuyama, in particular—announced that we had reached the "end of history." Nothing could be further from the truth. In fact, now that the bitter ideological confrontation sparked by this century's collision of "isms" has ended, larger numbers of people from more points on the globe than ever before have aggressively come forward to participate *in* history. They have left behind centuries, even millennia, of obscurity in forest and desert and rural isolation to request from the world community—and from the global economy that links it together—a decent life for themselves and a better life for their children. A generation ago, even a decade ago, most of them were as voiceless and invisible as they had always been. This is true no longer: they have entered history with a vengeance, and they have demands—economic demands—to make.

But to whom or to what should they make them? Their first impulse, of course, will likely be to turn to the heads of the governments of nation states. These, after all, are the leaders whose plans and schemes have long shaped the flow of public events. But, in

1

today's more competitive world, nation states no longer possess the seemingly bottomless well of resources from which they used to draw with impunity to fund their ambitions. These days, even they have to look for assistance to the global economy and make the changes at home needed to invite it in. So these new claimants will turn to international bodies like the United Nations. But what is the UN if not a collection of nation states? So they will turn to multilateral agencies like the World Bank, but these too are the creatures of a nation state-defined and -funded universe. So they will turn to explicitly economic groupings like OPEC or G-7 or ASEAN or APEC or NAFTA or the EU (European Union). But once again, all they will find behind each new acronym is a grouping of nation states.

Then, if they are clever, they may interrupt their quest to ask a few simple questions. Are these nation states—notwithstanding the obvious and important role they play in world affairs—really the primary actors in today's global economy? Do they provide the best window on that economy? Do they provide the best port of access to it? In a world where economic borders are progressively disappearing, are their arbitrary, historically accidental boundaries genuinely meaningful in economic terms? And if not, what kinds of boundaries do make sense? In other words, exactly what, at bottom, are the natural business units—the sufficient, correctly-sized and scaled aggregations of people and activities—through which to tap into that economy?

One way to answer these questions is to observe the flows of what I call the 4 "I's" that define it. First, the capital markets in most developed countries are flush with excess cash for investment. Japan, for example, has the equivalent of US $10 trillion stored away. Even where a country itself hovers close to bankruptcy, there is often a huge accumulation of money in pension funds and life insurance programs. The problem is that suitable—and suitably large—investment opportunities are not often available in the same geographies where this money sits. As a result, the capital markets have developed a wide variety of mechanisms to transfer it across national borders.[1] Today, nearly 10 percent of U.S. pension funds is invested in Asia. Ten years ago, that degree of participation in Asian markets would have been unthinkable.

Thus, investment—the first "I"—is no longer geographically constrained. Now, wherever you sit in the world, if the opportunity is attractive, the money will come in. And it will be, for the most part, "private" money. Again, ten years ago, the flow of cross-border funds was primarily from government to government or from multilateral lending agency to government. There was a capital city and an army of public bureaucrats on at least one end of the transaction. That is no longer the case. Because most of the money now moving across borders is private, governments do not have to be involved at either end. All that matters is the quality of the investment opportunity. The money will go where the good opportunities are.[2]

The second "I"—industry—is also far more global in orientation today than it was a decade ago. In the past, with the interests of their home governments clearly in mind, companies would strike deals with host governments to bring in resources and skills in exchange for privileged access to local markets. This, too, has changed. The strategies of modern multinational corporations are no longer shaped and conditioned by reasons of state but, rather, by the desire—and the need—to serve attractive markets wherever they exist and to tap attractive pools of resources wherever they sit. Government-funded subsidies—old-fashioned tax breaks for investing in this or that location—are becoming irrelevant as a decision criterion. The Western firms now moving, say, into parts of China and India are there because that is where their future lies, not because the host government has suddenly dangled a carrot in front of their nose.

As corporations move, of course, they bring with them working capital. Perhaps more important, they transfer technology and managerial know-how. These are not concessions to host governments; they are the essential raw materials these companies need to do their work. But they also bring something else. Pension fund money in the United States, for example, might look for decent China-related opportunities by scouting out the possibilities on the Shanghai stock exchange. The prospects thus identified, however, will be largely unfamiliar. Money managers will do their best to provide adequate research, but everyone will admit that relevant knowledge is limited. But if it is a GE or an IBM or a Unilever or a P&G that is building a presence in China, the markets back home and elsewhere in the developed world will know how to evaluate that. They will be more comfortable with it. And that, in turn, expands the range of capital markets on which these companies can draw for resources to be used in China.

The movement of both investment and industry has been greatly facilitated by the third "I"—information technology—which now makes it possible for a company to operate in various parts of the world without having to build up an entire business system in each of the countries where it has a presence. Engineers at workstations in Osaka can easily control plant operations in newly exciting parts of China like Dalian. Product designers in Oregon can control the activities of a network of factories throughout Asia-Pacific. Thus, the hurdles for cross-border participation and strategic alliance[3] have come way down. Armies of experts do not have to be transferred; armies of workers do not have to be trained. Capability can reside in the network and be made available—virtually anywhere—as needed.

Finally, individual consumers—the fourth "I"—have also become more global in orientation. With better access to information about lifestyles around the globe, they are much less likely to want to buy— and much less conditioned by government injunctions to buy—American or French or Japanese products merely because of their national associations. Consumers increasingly want the best and cheapest products, no matter where they come from. And they have shown their willingness to vote these preferences with their pocketbooks.

Taken together, the mobility of these four I's makes it possible for viable economic units in any part of the world to pull in whatever is needed for development. They need not look for assistance only to pools of resources close to home. Nor need they rely on the formal efforts of governments to attract resources from elsewhere and funnel them to the ultimate users. This makes the traditional "middleman" function of nation states—and of their governments—largely unnecessary. Because the global markets for all the I's work just fine on their own, nation states no longer have to play a market-making role. In fact, given their own troubles, which are considerable, they most often just get in the way. If allowed, global solutions will flow to where they are needed without the intervention of nation states. On current evidence, moreover, they flow better precisely because such intervention is absent.

This fundamentally changes the economic equation. If the unfettered movement of these I's makes the middleman role of nation states obsolete, the qualifications needed to sit at the global table and pull in global solutions begin to correspond not to the artificial political borders of countries, but to the more focused geographical units—Hong Kong, for example, and the adjacent stretch of southern China, or the Kansai region around Osaka, or Catalonia—where real work gets done and real markets flourish. I call these units "region states." They may lie entirely within or across the borders of a nation state. This does not matter. It is the irrelevant result of historical accident. What defines them is not the location of their political borders but the fact that they are the right size and scale to be the true, natural business units in today's global economy.[4] Theirs are the borders—and the connections—that matter in a borderless world.[5]

In the chapters that follow, I will show why traditional nation states have become unnatural, even impossible, business units in a global economy. I will also show why region states are, in fact, so effective as ports of entry to it. And I will explore how these developments change, deeply and forever, the logic that defines how corporations operate and how the governments of nation states understand their proper role in economic affairs.

Chapter One

THE CARTOGRAPHIC ILLUSION

A funny—and, to many observers, a very troubling—thing has happened on the way to former U.S. President Bush's so-called "new world order": the old world has fallen apart. Most visibly, with the ending of the Cold War, the long-familiar pattern of alliances and oppositions among industrialized nations has fractured beyond repair. Less visibly, but arguably far more important, the modern nation state itself—that artifact of the 18th and 19th centuries—has begun to crumble.

For many observers, this erosion of the long-familiar building blocks of the political world has been a source of discomfort at least and, far more likely, of genuine distress. They used to be confident that they could tell with certainty where the boundary lines ran. These are our people; those are not. These are our interests; those are not. These are our industries; those are not. It did not matter that little economic activity remained truly domestic in any sense that an Adam Smith or a David Ricardo would understand. Nor did it matter that the people served or the interests protected represented a small and diminishing fraction of the complex social universe within each set of established political borders.

The point, after all, was that everyone knew—or could talk and act as if he or she knew—where the boundary lines ran. Everyone's dealings could rest, with comfortable assurance, on the certain knowledge, as Robert Reich has put it, of who was "us" and who was "them." The inconvenient fact that most of the guns pointed in anger during the past two decades were pointed by national governments at some segment of the people those governments would define as "us"—well, that really did not matter, either. Boundaries are boundaries.

Politics, runs the time-worn adage, is the art of the possible. Translated, that means it is also the art of ignoring or overlooking discordant facts: guns pointed the wrong way, democratic institutions clogged to the point of paralysis by minority interests defended in the name of the majority—and, perhaps most important, domestic economies in an increasingly borderless world of economic activity. So what if average GNP per capita in China is $317 but, in Shenzhen, whose economy is closely linked with that of Hong Kong, it is $5,695? Boundaries are boundaries, and political dividing lines mean far more than demonstrable communities of economic interest.

No, they don't. Public debate may still be hostage to the outdated vocabulary of political borders, but the daily realities facing most people in the developed and developing worlds—both as citizens and as consumers—speak a vastly different idiom. Theirs is the language of an increasingly borderless economy, a true global marketplace. But the references we have—the maps and guides—to this new terrain are still largely drawn in political terms. Moreover, as the primary features on this landscape—the traditional nation states—begin to come apart at the seams, the overwhelming temptation is to redraw obsolete, U.N.-style maps to reflect the shifting borders of those states. The temptation is understandable, but the result is pure illusion. No more than the work of early cartographers do these new efforts show the boundaries and linkages that matter in the world now emerging. They are the product of illusion, and they are faithful to their roots.

This, too, is understandable. Much of the current awareness of the decay of the modern nation state has been driven by the wrenching experiences of the former Soviet Union and Czechoslovakia, which have formally ceased to exist as single national entities. Perhaps even more frightening, of course, is the noxious brew of ancient hatred, more recent antagonism, and unbridled ambition in what used to be Yugoslavia. These are extremes, to be sure, but they are deeply representative of the kind of erosion that has at last begun to capture an important share of public attention.

In a newly unified Germany, for example, unprecedented amounts of power have been ceded to the individual *Länder*.[1] In Canada, before the recent elections in Quebec and even before the failure of the Meech Lake accords, the French-speaking province had been moving to cut its constitutional ties with the other, English-speaking provinces.[2] In Spain, an explicit program of devolution is transferring much of the apparatus of independent statehood to the country's 17 "autonomous communities," especially those like Catalonia with a deeply entrenched historical identity of their own. In Italy, long-preoccupied with the problems of the Mezzagiorno in the south, recent elections have shown the Lombard League in the north to be a real and growing factor on the political scene.[3] Even in *dirigiste* France,[4] the prefects of Mitterrand's government can no longer unilaterally veto local decisions in the country's 22 provinces.

Developments as striking as these clearly merit the attention they have received in the media and in the regular comments of opinion makers and public officials. Nearly a half century of Cold War cannot end without dramatic—and eminently noteworthy—changes on both sides. Relaxation of the long-entrenched bipolar discipline imposed by the United States and the former USSR cannot help but allow even older fault lines to spread. Equally striking, however, is the way in which such attention has been framed and articulated. To the extent these developments have been treated as evidence of a systemic challenge to traditional nation states (and not just as a challenge to this or that current policy or set of leaders), they have been interpreted for the most part in political terms. Whatever their root, the centrifugal forces now at work have been seen to be meaningful, first and foremost, as statements about the inadequacies of established modes and processes of political order—that is, as evidence of troubling realignments within previously established borders.

Thus, as today's public debate would have it, the fission represented by local autonomy and by ethnic or racial or even tribal irredentism, no less than the proposed fusion represented by Maastricht, shows clearly that the postwar writ of central governments no longer holds with anything like the power it enjoyed even a generation ago.

And as that debate would also have it, this failure of the political center is a legitimate cause for concern. When no one seems to know where we are—or should be—going, initiative stagnates, special interests reduce each other to paralysis, and the consensus necessary for effective policy moves still further out of reach. In tones of despair, the more literary pundits like to cite Yeats: "Things fall apart; The center cannot hold." But the truer message comes from Matthew Arnold: we are "wandering between two worlds,/ One dead, the other unable to be born."

These lamentations at least have the virtue of taking the erosion of nation states seriously. But they view it almost entirely as the result of long-repressed political aspirations bursting into the open once the various imposed restraints of the Cold War era have been relaxed. No matter how deeply rooted, however, these aspirations are not the only—or arguably, even the primary—forces now at work. Something else is going on. The battle and the battlefield have shifted.

A QUESTION OF CULTURE?

In a recent, highly influential article, "The Clash of Civilizations?"[5] Samuel Huntington offers an interpretation of what that "something else" is. According to Huntington, the fault lines in our new, post-Cold War world do not flow from politics or ideology, but from culture. From now on, when large masses of people join in common purpose, the primary link between them will increasingly be their shared heritage of language, history, tradition, and religion—that is, civilization. And when they stonily face each other across a divide, the unbridgeable gap between them will be the lack of just such a shared civilization. Groupings based on culture will become—in fact, have already become—the most powerful actors in world affairs.

For all the truth of these observations, Huntington's argument ignores the fact that, even within the same civilization, people have often fought against each other. From the outside, the differences between Catholics and Protestants in Northern Ireland do not seem like a good reason for intense hatred. But for political leaders and mass agitators, they are good enough. Again, from outside, it is awfully difficult to tell the Hutu from the Tutsi in Rwanda. But they have mutually created, during the past decade, one of the bloodiest clashes in the world. People usually fight when their political and/or military leaders inflate minute differences so as to stir up latent hatred—not when "civilizations" clash. If leaders are enlightened, they can make their people believe in the power of working together. This is the case today with the multiple races and cultures linked peacefully by Lee Kwan Yew in Singapore and Dr. Mahathir in Malaysia (and was true in the Yugoslavia of Josip Broz Tito and the India of Mahatma Gandhi and Jawaharlal Nehru after World War II). It is not civilizations that promote clashes. They occur when old-fashioned leaders look for old-fashioned ways to solve problems by rousing their people to armed confrontation.

Such skirmishes confuse the ground of geopolitical interpretation. But they confuse the ground of economic interpretation as well. The glue holding together older constellations of nation-based political interests has visibly begun to wear thin. In economics as in politics, the older patterns of nation-to-nation linkage have begun to lose their dominance. What is emerging in their place, however, is not a set of new channels based on culture instead of nations. Nor is it a simple realignment of previous flows of nation-based trade or investment.

In my view, what is really at stake is not really which party or policy agenda dominates the apparatus of a nation state's central government. Nor is it the number of new, independent units into which that old center, which has held through the upheavals of industrialization and the agonies of two world wars, is likely to decompose. Nor is it the cultural fault lines along which it is likely to fragment.

Instead, what we are witnessing is the cumulative effect of fundamental changes in the currents of economic activity around the globe. So powerful have these currents become that they have carved out entirely new channels for themselves—channels that owe nothing to the lines of demarcation on traditional political maps. Put simply, in terms of real flows of economic activity, nation states have *already* lost their role as meaningful units of participation in the global economy of today's borderless world.

In the first place, these long-established, politically defined units have much less to contribute—and much less freedom to make contributions. The painful irony is that, driven by a concern to boost overall economic well-being, their efforts to assert traditional forms of economic sovereignty over the peoples and regions lying within their borders are now having precisely the opposite effect. Reflexive twinges of sovereignty make the desired economic success impossible, because the global economy punishes twinging countries by diverting investment and information elsewhere.

The uncomfortable truth is that, in terms of the global economy, nation states have become little more than bit actors. They may originally have been, in their mercantilist phase, independent, powerfully efficient engines of wealth creation. More recently, however, as the downward-ratcheting logic of electoral politics has placed a death grip on their economies, they have become—first and foremost—remarkably inefficient engines of wealth distribution. Elected political leaders gain and keep power by giving voters what they want, and what they want rarely entails a substantial decrease in the benefits, services, or subsidies handed out by the state.

Moreover, as the workings of genuinely global capital markets dwarf their ability to control exchange rates or protect their currency, nation states have become inescapably vulnerable to the discipline imposed by economic choices made elsewhere by people and institutions over which they have no practical control. Witness, for example, the recent, Maastricht-related bout of speculation against the franc, the pound, and the kronor. Witness, also, the unsustainable but self-imposed burden of Europe's various social programs. Finally, witness the complete absence of any economic value creation, save for those around the world who stand to benefit from pork-barrel excesses, in such decisions as the Japanese Diet's commitment—copied from the New Deal policies of Franklin Roosevelt—to build unnecessary highways and bridges on the remote islands of Hokkaido and Okinawa.

Second, and more to the point, the nation state is increasingly a nostalgic fiction. It makes even less sense today, for example, than it did a few years ago to speak of Italy or Russia or China[6] as a single economic unit. Each is a motley combination of territories with vastly different needs and vastly different abilities to contribute. For a private sector manager or a public sector official to treat them as if they represented a single economic entity is to operate on the basis of demonstrably false, implausible, and nonexistent averages. This may still be a political necessity, but it is a bald-faced economic lie.

Third, when you look closely at the goods and services now produced and traded around the world, as well as at the companies responsible for them, it is no easy matter to attach to them an accurate national label. Is an automobile sold under an American marque really a U.S. product when a large percentage of its components comes from abroad?[7] Is the performance of IBM's foreign subsidiaries or the performance of its R&D operations in Europe and Japan really a measure of U.S. excellence in technology?[8] For that matter, are the jobs created by Japanese plants and factories in the Mississippi Valley really a measure of the health of the Japanese, and not the U.S., economy?[9] The barbershop on the corner may indisputably be a part of the domestic American economy. But it is just not possible to make the same claim, with the same degree of confidence, about the firms active on the global stage.[10]

Finally, when economic activity aggressively wears a national label these days, that tag is usually present neither for the sake of accuracy nor out of concern for the economic well-being of individual consumers. It is there primarily as a mini-flag of cheap nationalism—that is, as a jingoistic celebration of nationhood that places far more value on emotion-grabbing symbols than on real, concrete improvements in quality of life.[11] By contrast, we don't hear much about feverish waves of Hong Kong nationalism, but the people in Hong Kong seem to live rather well.[12] With much fanfare, Ukraine and the Baltic states have now become independent, but do their people have more food to eat or more energy to keep them warm during the winter or more electricity for light to see by?

An arresting, if often overlooked, fact about today's borderless economy is that people often have better access to low-cost, high-quality products when they are not produced "at home." Singaporeans, for example, enjoy better and cheaper agricultural products than do the Japanese, although Singapore has no farmers—and no farms—of its own.[13] Much the same is true of construction materials, which are much less expensive in Singapore, which produces none of them, than in Japan, which does.

Now, given this decline in the relevance of nation states as units of economic activity, as well as the recent burst of economic growth in Asia, the burgeoning political self-consciousness of Islam, and the fragmentation, real or threatened, of such "official" political entities as Italy, Spain, Somalia, Rwanda, Canada, South Africa, and the former Yugoslavia, Czechoslovakia, and Soviet Union—given all this, it is easy to see why observers like Huntington should look to cultural, religious, ethnic, even tribal affiliations as the only plausible stopping point of the centrifugal forces unleashed by the end of the Cold War.

Once bipolar discipline begins to lose its force, once traditional nation states no longer "hold," or so the argument goes, visionless leaders will start to give in to the fear that older fault lines will again make themselves felt. And given the bloody violence with which many of these lines have already begun to reappear, these leaders will find it hard to see where this process of backsliding can come to rest short of traditional groupings based on some sort of cultural affinity. In other words, in the absence of vision and the presence of slowly rising panic, the only groupings that seem to matter are based on civilizations, not nations.

But are cultures or civilizations meaningful aggregates in terms of which to understand economic activity? Think, for a moment, of the ASEAN countries. In what sense is it useful to talk about them as a single, culturally defined economic area? As they affect local patterns of work, trade, and industry, the internal differences among their Buddhist, Islamic, Catholic (in the Philippines and the Sabah state of Malaysia), and Confucian traditions are every bit as large as, if not larger than, the differences separating any one of these traditions from the dominant business cultures of New York or London or Paris.

But in ASEAN, at least, differences of this sort do not provoke the same kinds of conflicts that often arise elsewhere. Most Western observers know, for example, that Spanish and Portuguese speakers can converse with each other, if with some minor degree of difficulty. Many fewer, however, know that the same is true of Indonesians and Malaysians. Or that, in border regions between Thailand and Malaysia, such as Phuket, there are peaceful, economically linked villages, some of which have mainly Buddhist and some mainly Islamic populations. These on-the-ground realities have made it possible for ASEAN leaders to accept and to reinforce, with little fear of internal friction, the development of cross-border economic ties like those stretching across the

Strait of Malacca which are represented by the Greater Growth Triangle of Phuket, Medan, and Penang.

Even more important than such cultural differences within a civilization, and what Huntington's line of thought leaves out, is the issue of historical context. The particular dissolution of bipolar, "great power" discipline that so greatly affects us today is not taking place in the 1790s or the 1890s, but the 1990s. And that means it is taking place in a world whose peoples, no matter how far-flung geographically or disparate culturally, are all linked to much the same sources of global information. The immediacy and completeness of their access may vary, of course, and governments may try to impose restrictions and control. Even if they do, however, the barriers will not last forever, and leakages will occur all along the way. Indeed, the basic fact of linkage to global flows of information is a—perhaps, *the*—central, distinguishing fact of our moment in history. Whatever the civilization to which a particular group of people belongs, they now get to hear about the way other groups of people live, the kinds of products they buy, the changing focus of their tastes and preferences as consumers, and the styles of life they aspire to lead.

But they also get something more. For more than a decade, some of us have been talking about the progressive globalization of markets for consumer goods like Levi's jeans, Nike athletic shoes, and Hermés scarves—a process, driven by global exposure to the same information, the same cultural icons, and the same advertisements, that I have elsewhere referred to as the "California-ization" of taste.[14] Today, however, the process of convergence goes faster and deeper. It reaches well beyond taste to much more fundamental dimensions of worldview, mind-set, and even thought process. There are now, for example, tens of millions of teenagers around the world who, having been raised in a multimedia-rich environment, have a lot more in common with each other than they do with members of older generations in their own cultures. For these budding consumers, technology-driven convergence does not take place at the sluggish rate dictated by yesterday's media. It is instantaneous—a nanosecond migration of ideas and innovations.

The speed and immediacy of such migrations take us over an invisible political threshold. In the post-Cold War world, the information flows underlying economic activity in virtually all corners of the globe simply cannot be maintained as the possession of private elites or public officials. They are shared, increasingly, by all citizens and consumers. This sharing does not, of course, imply any necessary similarity in how local economic choices finally get made. But it does imply that there is a powerful centripetal force at work, counteracting and counterbalancing all the centrifugal forces noted above.

The emotional nexus of culture, in other words, is not the only web of shared interest able to contain the processes of disintegration unleashed by the reappearance of older fault lines. Information-driven participation in the global economy can do so, too, ahead of the fervid but empty posturing of both cheap nationalism and cultural messianism. The well-informed citizens of a global marketplace will not wait passively until nation states or cultural prophets deliver tangible improvements in lifestyle. They no longer trust them to do so. Instead, they want to build their own future, now, for themselves and by themselves. They want their own means of direct access to what has become a genuinely global economy.

INCONVENIENT AVERAGES

What this combination of forces at last makes clear is that the nation state has become an unnatural—even a dysfunctional—organizational unit for thinking about economic activity. It combines things at the wrong level of aggregation.

What sense does it make, for example, to think of Italy as a coherent economic entity within the EU? There is no "average" Italy.[15] There is no large social or economic group precisely at the midpoint represented by such averages, no constituency specially advantaged by—and, therefore, eager to support—split-the-difference political compromises. There is, instead, an industrial north and a rural south, which are vastly different in their ability to contribute and their need to receive. In economic terms, there is simply no justification for treating Italy as a single-interest entity. Doing so forces you—as private sector manager or public sector official—to operate on the basis of false, implausible, and inconvenient averages. They are a fiction, and a destructive fiction at that.

But the root problem goes deeper. In a borderless economy, any statistical regime that takes the nation state as its primary unit of analysis is—and must be—badly out of date. For well over a decade now, I have been arguing just this point in the context of the perennial squabbles between Japan and the United States on questions of trade and trade balances.[16] On both sides, however, most officials and even most commentators remain perversely afflicted with trade blindness[17]—an inability to see, let alone understand, in the broad daylight of media attention, the core facts about cross-border economic activity.

Position papers and headlines notwithstanding, the trade problem between Japan and the United States is neither the American trade deficit nor the Japanese surplus. The reason is quite simple: the flows of activity measured by official trade statistics[18] represent a tiny and steadily diminishing share of the economic linkages between the two countries. These data, remember, do not count the revenues from services, licenses, or intellectual property, or from goods manufactured by U.S. firms in third countries but sold in Japan, or from goods both manufactured and sold in Japan by U.S. firms. All they count is that relatively small universe of things physically produced in the United States, crated, loaded onto ships or planes, passed through customs, and then uncrated and sold in Japan.[19]

When a U.S. software house sells its leading-edge program in Tokyo, the trade data capture little, if any, of the value added. When a U.S. chip manufacturer sells its products in Osaka, the sales may count toward the 20 percent of the market earmarked for U.S. firms, but—if the chips were, as is likely, actually produced in Malaysia—they will not show up in U.S. export statistics. When a U.S. sportswear company retails in Hokkaido garments sewn in Indonesia or Taiwan, the sales do not matter to those who count bilateral trade flows. When enough Japanese consumers see a U.S. movie to generate, say, US $200 million in box office revenues and, perhaps, US $40 million in royalties, these figures show up in Japan's current account, but not in its trade statistics. But if the moviemaker "sold" each copy of the film to be shown in Japan for US $1 million, those monies would count as trade revenue.[20]

As everyone should know by now, the official statistics that attract so much political attention are unreliable. I'm being polite: they are an out-and-out falsehood. They are not an accurate reflection of real flows of economic activity. They are not an accurate reflection of anything. Indeed, in the mid-1980s, if you included in these official numbers all the sales in Japan of "American" (as consumers perceive them) goods and services, you would find that the Japanese bought—per capita—four times as much "American" stuff as Americans bought "Japanese" stuff.[21] Since then, the ratio has only gotten larger.

Trade, however, is only the most visible of the areas in which official, nation state-based statistics prove their worthlessness. The list is long and varied. Some countries, for example, classify life insurance as savings; in others, it is an expense. Some treat government-funded pensions as part of individual income; others, as a public liability. Some view mortgage investment in a home as consumption; others, as a form of savings. Some categorize devices like microwave ovens as white goods; others, as consumer electronics or even furniture. At even the simplest level, therefore, meaningful comparisons are hard to come by. Apples and oranges are not the problem. It's fruit salad.

These differences matter. In the mid-1980s—in 1986, to take a particular example[22]—the official Japanese domestic savings rate was 16.6 percent; the U.S. rate was 4.3 percent. The result: loud and acrimonious debate between the two countries, with the United States calling on Japan to boost domestic consumption and Japan insisting that the United States get its own fiscal house in order by reducing wasteful, deficit-financed consumption. These charges and countercharges continue to fly. Neither then nor now, however, do they bear much relation to the underlying facts: the savings rate in both countries is pretty much the same.

Japanese data on savings, like those for most other countries, are based on a System of National Accounts (SNA) advocated by the United Nations. By contrast, the U.S. data are based on National Income and Product Accounts (NIPA), which are administered by the Department of Commerce. Converting from NIPA to SNA would boost the 1986 U.S. savings rate from 4.3 percent to 6.8 percent. This is a substantial jump, to be sure, but still far less than Japan's 16.6 percent. If you also removed the other structural inconsistencies between SNA and NIPA—the differing treatments of government social insurance, for example, which SNA views as personal savings and NIPA as government savings—the 6.8 percent figure would rise further to 10.9 percent. And much of the remaining 5.7 percentage point gap (16.6 percent v. 10.9 percent) would disappear if you corrected for essentially social differences between the two countries.

In the United States, for example, if you buy a house for $200,000 and invest the same amount again in renovation, the government counts the first number as savings and the second as consumption. When you sell the house, of course, you hope to get at least $400,000 for it, which effectively equates overall resale value with savings. In Japan, however, where renovations are usually not appreciated by later buyers and only land is treated as having real value, the equivalent of $200,000 spent on fixing things up truly is consumption.

There are still other adjustments to be made. Americans tend to buy on credit; the Japanese, given low resale values, "save to buy." Adding savings to consumer credit in both countries gives roughly the same number: 29 percent of disposable income. The only difference is the timing of payment: the Japanese buy later, thus showing more money in the bank at present; Americans buy now and pay later, thus borrowing from the future. Moreover, for major purchases like homes, Japanese banks require a much larger down payment than their U.S. counterparts. If, in addition to the other adjustments noted above, Japan's banks were to reduce their requirements to the low end of the U.S. spectrum—say, 10 percent or so of the down payment—virtually all of the statistical "savings gap" between the two countries would disappear. The numbers everyone knows and everyone uses are simply untrue.

So, it is not culture that produces the huge statistical differences between the Americans and the Japanese. It is the differences in their systems—taxation, say, or banking on the statistical treatment of things like pensions—that collectively make the two peoples behave very differently. Certainly, the Japanese are not by nature more hardworking or more inclined to save than the Americans. The crucial point, of course, is that if these systems were changed, both would behave pretty much the same.

The evidence, then, is as exhaustive as it is uncomfortable: in a borderless economy, the nation-focused maps we typically use to make sense of economic activity are woefully misleading. We must, managers and policymakers alike, face up at last to the awkward and uncomfortable truth: the old cartography no longer works. It has become no more than an illusion.

Chapter Two

THE LADDER OF DEVELOPMENT

Even at the most literal level, as the previous chapter shows, there is not much evidence to support the notion that economic activity in today's borderless world follows either the political boundary lines of traditional nation states or the cultural boundary lines of what Huntington calls "civilizations." But there is plenty of evidence that it does follow information-driven efforts to participate in the global economy. Such efforts, moreover, tend not to happen at random—that is, there is a fairly predictable trajectory along which priorities shift as economic areas move through successive phases of development. This movement up the ladder of development has nothing to do with culture and everything to do with a region's ability to put the right policies, institutions, and infrastructure in place at the right time.

At around the equivalent of US $3,000 per capita of GNP, there is usually a strong but steady increase in the desire to achieve more active involvement with the global economy, both as a market and as a source of supply for basic consumer goods. (In Japan, for example, this took the form of rapidly expanding consumer demand for refrigerators, color TVs, and low-cost automobiles.)[1] Below this level—between, say, US $1,500 and $3,000 per capita—the emphasis is more on motorbikes (as it is today in Thailand); below US $1,500, it is more on bicycles (as in Shanghai and Vietnam). At the US $3,000

21

threshold, therefore, it makes sense to begin serious construction of modern highway systems, of rail transportation systems in major urban areas, and of the nonamenity-focused infrastructure—drinking water, electric power, communications, and finance—needed to support a significantly higher level of international commerce.

At the US $5,000 threshold, things change yet again. The strength of the wish to be part of the global economic system escalates rapidly. Later, at US $10,000, the symbol of achievement is joining the OECD. At this midpoint, however, the symbol of choice seems to be hosting the Olympic Games. Although the Mexico City Olympics of 1968 took place just as the country passed the $3,000 level, Japan passed the $5,000 marker in 1965, a year after it hosted the Tokyo Olympics. More recently, the Seoul Olympics of 1988 reflected South Korea's having just passed the $5,000 level.

At this stage of development, the demand for quality automobiles takes off, as does the need for up-to-date international airports and a high-speed railway system. (In Japan, the first major highway between Tokyo and Haneda Airport opened just a few weeks before the 1964 games.) At this stage, also, it often happens that the drive for even greater material prosperity begins to crowd out, even for local elites, quality of life considerations, which tend not to return in force until GNP moves well beyond the $10,000 level. One common result is that air and water pollution rapidly become unbearable, and governments have to begin making the infrastructure investments to reduce them. If they wait too long, the price tag for correcting these excesses down the road in a thoroughly built-up industrial environment can easily become intolerable. But they may not even have the luxury, albeit mistaken, to wait. The more advanced industrial economies with which they trade may require such remedial actions as the price of admission to developed country status.

But there is something that usually does not happen at $5,000: although linkages with the global economy expand, the "softer" aspects of the economy (the currency, as well as banking and communications, for example) do not open up. The heavy hand of government regulation and control remains pretty firmly in place. The temptation, of course, is to leave things as they are. After all, why face the disruption and loss of control that a deregulated and open economy would bring? Most midsized countries in Europe have given in to this temptation, which explains the sluggishness with which they have struggled beyond the $5,000 barrier. By contrast, Taiwan,[2] at a comparable point in its development, aggressively moved to deregulate foreign exchange and many other markets. As a result, its economy shot up to the $10,000 level in only a few years. Singapore did basically the same thing. So did Hong Kong, which explains why its economy shot by the $5,000 barrier and Korea's did not, although it had competed neck-to-neck with Korea until that point.[3]

The evidence is clear: what a government does at $5,000 makes a huge difference to how quickly—and how well—it can join the $10,000 club. As long as reasonably sensible policies are in place, if it makes use of—that is, if it genuinely opens itself up to—the global system, prosperity follows. If it does not or if it does so only half-heartedly, choosing to rely instead on the heavy, guiding hand of central government control, its progress will falter.

Japan is something of an exception to this. As we were making our way by the usual route toward the $10,000 threshold, our unusual degree of energy-dependence caused us to focus on creating very energy-efficient products. Moreover, lacking a well-developed highway system, our companies decided to test on California highways the small cars we had designed primarily for our domestic market. Thus, Japanese cars just happened to be available in the United States when the energy crisis of 1973 hit, and American consumers responded with unprecedented enthusiasm—and their checkbooks. There was no planning. It was pure, dumb luck.

Then came the collapse of the Bretton Woods Agreement, which forced us—ready or not—to open up our currency market. (The stock, bond, and property markets, of course, lagged behind.) Dumb luck again. Given the importance of our financial markets and given the radiating connections between the automobile and many other critical industries—electronics, steel, chemicals, batteries, tires, corrosion protection, and so on—these happy strokes of luck quickly pulled us beyond the $10,000 barrier, even though government still had not relaxed its close control of the economy.

In the mid-1980s, after the Plaza Agreement of 1985 allowed the value of the dollar to fall, a rapidly appreciating yen boosted Japan's per capita GNP to the $20,000 level (in dollar terms) with unseemly haste. At that time, the yen/dollar exchange rate was at 265. Today, with Japan at the US $30,000 level, the yen is below 100. In both cases, we broke through to new GNP thresholds not so much because of anything we had done as because of events over which we had no control. It is the magic of currency exchange, not of clear-sighted economic policy, that has made our performance, as measured by dollar-denominated GNP per capita, number one in the world. Our yen-based income has not risen appreciably since the Plaza accord.

This is both a blessing and a curse. The blessing is obvious. The curse is that we managed to build a truly world-class economy without our government's being forced to relax its grip and lead industry through a sustained, systematic process of deregulation. Today, as a result, we have a $30,000 economy, but a government mind-set—and skill level—better suited to a nation on the verge of cracking the $10,000 ceiling.[4]

No wonder consumer frustrations mount and trade frictions with the United States multiply. The countries are speaking languages relevant to vastly different stages of economic development. Although purchasing power parity (PPP) calculations would put the "right" exchange rate of the yen at about 190 to the dollar, a stubborn automobile industry-led trade surplus has pushed it below the 100 mark. This penalizes consumers and needlessly irritates trade relations. The nearly factor-of-two difference is direct evidence of what happens when a government is slow to adjust its economic system to the logic of the global marketplace. If the Japanese government deregulated and otherwise opened up domestic markets, consumers would benefit and PPP-based exchange rates would find their proper balance.

The Japanese situation notwithstanding, the point to remember about this notional GNP ladder is that it does apply, across dividing lines defined by culture, to all developing economies. The pull of the global economy, coupled with a growing ability to use that connection to move up along the ladder's various stages, is universal—and universally attractive. In a world where manufacturers often discount their prices for hardware by 20 percent or more and the average logistics costs of moving a product around the globe are less than 10 percent of its end-user price (TVs, for example, are 7 percent, and automobiles less than 5 percent), physical distance has become economically irrelevant. Economic borders have meaning, if at all, not as the dividing lines between civilizations or nation states, but as the contours of information flow. Where information reaches, demand grows; where demand grows, the global economy has a local home.

Chapter Three

THE NEW "MELTING POT"

Day to day, for more than twenty years, I have worked with senior managers in all parts of the Triad (Japan, Europe, and the United States), and in the newly industrialized economies of Asia, on the most important strategic issues facing their corporations. During that time, as I have described elsewhere in more detail (see, for example, *Triad Power,*[1] *Beyond National Borders,*[2] and *The Borderless World*),[3] there has been a fundamental change in the environment within which those managers work. At the heart of that discontinuity is a series of related developments in information technology.

Taken together, these developments have had three broad effects. First, at the macroeconomic level, they have made it possible for capital to be shifted instantaneously anywhere in the world. This means both that capital flows no longer need be tied to the physical movement of goods and that, by extension, the traditional forms of trade represent only a minute and decreasing fraction of cross-border economic activity. Second, at the company level, they have changed what managers can know in real time about their markets, products, and organizational processes. This means managers can be far more responsive to what their customers want and far more flexible in how they organize to make and provide it. Third, at the market level, these developments have changed what customers everywhere can know

27

about the way other people live, about the products and services available to them, and about the relative value such offerings provide. This means that economic nationalism exerts an ever-smaller influence on purchase decisions.

Whichever the country, when customers walk into a store, they both demand and expect to get the best and the cheapest—that is, the highest-value—products and services available. Indeed, consumers around the world are beginning to develop similar cultural expectations about what they ought to be able to buy as well as about what it is they want to buy. From São Paulo to Singapore, this process of convergence, which I have described elsewhere as the "Californiaization" of taste and preference,[4] is making today's "global" consumers more like each other in many respects than they are like either their nonglobally-oriented neighbors or their parents or grandparents.

A CROSS-BORDER CIVILIZATION

On old economic maps, the most important cartographic facts had to do with things like the location of raw material deposits, energy sources, navigable rivers, deep-water ports, railroad lines, paved roads—and national borders. On today's maps, by contrast, the most salient facts are the footprints cast by TV satellites, the areas covered by radio signals, and the geographic reach of newspapers and magazines. Information has replaced both propinquity and politics as the factor most likely to shape the flows of economic activity. Physical terrain and political boundaries still matter, of course, but neither—and especially not political boundaries—matters as much as what people know or want or value.

In a sense, the intangibles of local knowledge, taste, and preference have always played a critical shape-giving role. Long before nation states existed, long before the cities, towns, and villages out of which they grew took recognizable form, groups of people linked by social and cultural ties regularly exchanged what they could hunt, fish, grow, gather, extract, or make. The meaningful horizons of their lives were circumscribed not by the artifice of formal political institutions, but by the land on which they lived and the social webs that enclosed them. Even in the modern world, with its crazy quilt of political borders,

hundreds of millions of people—rural peasants, for example, in remote areas of China—exist in much the same fashion. Political dividing lines got added late, indeed, to these venerable maps of local
experience. The ink is barely dry.

Even so, it is fading. And it is fading ever more quickly. Better information, made possible by better technology, is the reason. As the
quality, range, and availability of information improve, growing numbers of people—no matter what their geographical location—come to
know in ever finer detail how other people in other places live. At the
same time, they come to know what kinds of economic choices can
be made and what levels of value attach to those choices. Such knowledge and awareness, in turn, inevitably work to undermine the tyranny of both physical distance and government edict. The larger the
field of known possibilities, the harder it is for a central authority to
limit that field arbitrarily—or to make those limitations stick.

Centuries ago, the first Western travelers to reach Asia returned
with goods and spices and artworks that forever changed the universe
of possibilities out of which tastes and preferences at home would
later crystallize. On this road of discovery, there is no going back. Or
going more slowly. Indeed, in recent years, when the Silk Road is no
longer a dangerous route through uncharted terrain but merely a degree of access to global media, like Fox TV, the time required for exposure to new dimensions of choice has shrunk to virtually nothing. And
the barriers to such exposure have either disappeared or proven endlessly porous.

Even given the irreducibly local portion in any mix of customs and
preferences, a newly shared knowledge of what is possible cannot
help but lead across geographies to at least a partial convergence of
tastes and preferences. Global brands of blue jeans, colas, and stylish
athletic shoes are as much on the mind of the taxi driver in Shanghai
as they are in the kitchen or the closet of the schoolteacher in Stock-
holm or São Paulo.

For several decades now, this process of California-ization has provided much of the market-driven support for the development of a
genuinely borderless global economy.[5] But this kind of convergence,
important as it is, goes only so far. It overlays new tastes on an established, but largely unaffected, base of social norms and values. It adds

new elements to the local mix of goods and services, but leaves the worldview of the people who purchase them unchanged. It expands the universe of what is desirable, but does nothing to shift the fundamental mind-set of those who experience those pangs of desire. The contents of kitchens and closets may change, but the core mechanisms by which cultures maintain their identity and socialize their young remain untouched. Political borders may offer little meaningful resistance to invasion by new constellations of consumer taste, but social borders limit their scope and effectively quarantine them within the superficial layers of culture.

But this, too, is now beginning to change. Even social borders are starting to give way to the information- and technology-driven processes of convergence that have already turned political borders into largely meaningless lines on economic maps. There are two reasons for this. First, as societies move up the economic ladder of development past the US $5,000 per capita threshold, there is a notable upward ratcheting in the speed with which the lifestyles of their people—what they see and hear, what they buy, how they spend their time—grow more and more alike. The effects of this flywheel-like acceleration reach, to some extent, into the underlying nexus of culture. Some rough threshold does exist beyond which changes in degree of shared lifestyle become changes in kind of attitude and orientation.

Second, and more important, this acceleration is taking place at a moment in history when the very nature of the media exposure driving it is itself undergoing radical change. The multimedia experiences increasingly made possible by new technology have consequences that go far beyond surface issues of taste (and their implications for culture) to fundamental issues of thought process and mind-set. In those societies open to the influence of multimedia, the critical balance is already beginning to shift: children and teenagers are, at deep levels of sensibility and worldview, becoming much more like their counterparts in other societies similarly influenced than they are like the older generations within their own cultures. The essential continuity between generations, on which every society necessarily depends for its integrity and survival, has begun to fray. This fraying—this tilting of the balance—can, perhaps, be most clearly seen in the context of the recent social history of Japan.[6]

LIKE FATHER, LIKE . . . ?

The central fact about Japanese citizens in their 60s is that they experienced World War II. Either they participated in it directly, or they suffered from its indirect effects. Then they went out and, from the ashes of defeat, built the institutions and industries of a remarkably successful postwar Japan. To them, the quality of life they have been able to create is like heaven. Endless, unquestioned toil and hard work do not matter. They accept both without complaint as the perfectly tolerable price of a safe and secure existence. The military pretensions of great power status, however, they do not accept, for all things military represent a threat to everything they have so painstakingly built. They are, with precious few exceptions, pacifist in word and deed.

When this generation now in its 60s began its work of reconstruction, its commitment to sustained hard work carried the explicit—and entirely credible—promise of an attractive lifestyle in return. If they held up their end, they could live in a reasonable (and reasonably priced) fashion, could legitimately aspire to own their own extended family-sized homes, could reach their jobs in major urban areas with a commute of no more than 30 or 40 minutes, and could look forward to a decent standard of living after retirement, with at least some of their children and grandchildren living nearby (or with them) to look after their needs. For the generation now in its 50s and late 40s, however, none of this is true.

This middle-aged generation also knew the hunger and poverty of immediate postwar Japan, but was too young to take part in the rebuilding process—or in the full range of the promise it held out for improving personal lifestyles. They were brought up, in effect, by Douglas MacArthur: their formative years in school took place during the occupation. This had its benefits. Compared with their parents and grandparents, these individuals were exposed, early on, to a remarkably cosmopolitan view of the world. But it also had its costs. The message they heard, day after day, was that their country was a completely defeated, third-rate power—a power, moreover, that had done so much harm to its neighbors that the best thing it could now do was to disengage from the rest of the world and leave everyone else alone. In the world of the victors, their country was—as each of them

71975

was—a mere child, the U.N. was a benevolent though demanding uncle, and the United States was the all-powerful parent from whom all good things came.

After the formal occupation by the U.S. troops ended, the Japan-U.S. Security Treaty took effect in April of 1952. The treaty granted the United States the right to maintain military bases, first to keep watch for possible rearmament and later, as a forward line of defense against the Soviet Union's expansionist impulses in Asia. For the now middle-aged generation, the debate leading up to the ratification of this treaty throughout the 1960s was every bit as divisive a political and cultural issue as Vietnam was for its counterpart in America. It nearly tore the country apart. At a minimum, it forced this generational cohort, the *zenkyoto,* to think long and hard about the world and about the future security of the country. It pushed many into the arms of strongly leftist, even communist ideologies. And as the Vietnam War itself heated up, the fear that the U.S. bases might make Japan itself a target for Soviet nuclear missiles only added fuel to the domestic firestorm of protest already raging.

Even those Americans who grew up with the nightly media coverage of bloodshed in Vietnam and protest at home have, as a rule, little sense of how troubled and violent those years were in Japan. During the late 1960s and early 1970s, there were endless public demonstrations, during which quite a few people got killed, including Michiko Kambara, the daughter of a well-known professor. At Tokyo University, Yasuda Auditorium was burned down. Think of what happened at Kent State University and then imagine it many times worse, more sustained, and more violent. Imagine it, as well, taking place not just at one or two universities, but all across the nation. Further imagine these forces of protest as legitimately having—and at the time as being seen to have—the power to topple the national government. Countless numbers of students put off their careers and opted to stay on or about campus to be part of the action. The battles with the authorities were real, the stakes were real, the bloodshed was real.

In the aftermath, these leftist groups pretty much turned in on themselves and spent most of the rest of the 1970s in internecine battles. Their protest became a minor event. During the late 1960s, however, it was a major public event, nationwide. But its long-term effects on the generation that is now middle-aged proved curiously limited. When, after a delay, they finally made their way as salarymen into the regular work force, they seemed to forget their urgent social and political concerns about the world and about their own country. Like many of their counterparts in the United States, they simply buckled down to work—in effect, as the bag carriers of the men now in their 60s.

But the implicit "deal" such work offered had grown substantially less attractive. Commuting to work now took longer, as salarymen had to move further and further away from downtown areas to find affordable housing. The houses themselves were smaller and could no longer accommodate three-generation families. Their post-retirement prospects were much less certain. With their families now physically separated, who would look after them in their old age? Because they had reached the station a little bit late, the reliable train to the good life had already left. Their children would not even have a chance to catch it.

One possible response, of course, given roughly two decades of patient labor, was to accept this diminution of fortune in quiet frustration and disillusion. Another, however, was to recall the more active days of their young adulthood and, after a long delay, to again make their voices heard on social and political matters. Increasingly, these people are making this latter choice. This is the generation now most solidly behind the call for domestic reform. To them, special-interest gridlock in the government is not acceptable. The extortionate demands of the farmers are not acceptable. The pacifist and defeatist policies on the international stage of the men in their 60s and 70s are not acceptable. Though they have come to the party late, the men and women of *zenkyoto* still believe they can—and, more and more, that they must—change the world in which they and their children live.

The generation just behind them, however, the people in their mid-30s to mid-40s, see things quite differently. They are, in effect, Japan's "lost" generation. Their lives have never been marred by abject want or poverty. They have never known anything other than the firm, paternal hand of the Liberal Democratic Party (LDP) at the tiller of government. Their university years were not a period of social protest, but a temporary lull before careers as housewives or salarymen. What they had was not bad, and they had no experience in challenging authority or finding fault with the status quo. True, their residences were now only large enough for a tiny nuclear family at best, and their commute to work now took an hour and a half or more. But their response has largely been to keep their heads down and make the best of it.

To the next generation, the "angry young men and women" in their mid-20s to mid-30s, this inward-looking passivity seems no more than small-minded selfishness. They do not respect their immediate elders, whom they view as cowardly message carriers and not as creative, future-minded leaders. Yet this latter group blocks their advancement into positions where they could take more active responsibility for things.

Waiting patiently for their turn, however, is not a particularly tolerable option, because the bubble economy of the late 1980s effectively put an attractive quality of life out of reach. The maximum these young people will be able to spend on a house is 35 million yen or so, and even that will lock them into a commute of two hours or more each way. If they want to live only an hour from work, the kind of space they can afford—roughly 50 square meters—will give them minimal personal privacy and virtually no room to raise children. No wonder they are angry.

At the same time, however, they are actively exploring novel ways to build a pleasant life for themselves. If they cannot manage decent housing at home, why not allocate discretionary income, denominated in a strong yen, to vacation trips—and buying trips—abroad? Indeed, fully 97 percent of newly married couples in this cohort now take their honeymoons outside the country, mostly in Hawaii, California, Australia's Gold Coast, or Europe. By contrast, only 3 percent of the middle-aged generation went overseas for their honeymoons. The Japan in which they have grown up is, on a statistical basis, extremely affluent. But their only real chance to participate meaningfully in that affluence is through one or another form of escapism.

Foreign travel, of course, is only the most obvious expression of this. More important in its effects, but less obvious to foreign observers, is the addiction of this age group to publications like *Shonen Jump,* a cartoon-like magazine with a weekly circulation of six million and an editorial content modeled on the Harlequin romances so popular in the United States. What the stories in *Shonen Jump* tell them over and over again in countless different ways is that friends matter more than family, that nothing comes to the individual who refuses to make the needed effort, and that such efforts—if successful—bring not glorious victories, but small moments of personal satisfaction: a date with the prettiest girl or the handsomest boy in the class, a happy day windsurfing at the beach, a good evening spent talking with friends over tasty food and drink. Dreams of happiness, such as they are, are small, transient, intensely personal, and have nothing to do with family, society, or country.

Between this generation and the one immediately preceding it the nexus of social continuity is stretched thinner and finer than between any pair of generations discussed so far. In the world of *Shonen Jump*, family, parents, school, community, and country are all unpleasant distractions from the small pleasures of life. They are all unwelcome— and avoidable—sources of intrusive authority. They destroy the little possibility for happiness that does still exist. Much better, therefore, to ignore them, to refuse to accept the value systems they represent, and to go one's own way with one's friends.

THE NINTENDO KIDS

But even this fraying of the bonds of social continuity plays out, for the most part, within a distinctively Japanese cultural environment. To be sure, the world of *Shonen Jump* quietly ignores a number of traditional Japanese values, but it respects many others as well: the aesthetic pleasures to be found in small things, for example, or the importance of thoughtful interpersonal courtesies. Between this generation and the cohort of 15- to 25-year-olds, however, the web of continuity is stretched thin enough to finally break.

The differences here are fundamental. The relevant changes are not just in degree but in kind, and they go beyond surface issues of value to the underlying realities of mind-set and thought process. This is because the younger group came of age in a heavily multimedia-influenced environment: in Japan's 67 million households, there are now more than 30 million Nintendo and Sega "famicom" game machines. The inevitable result: the first true generation of "Nintendo kids."

The profound cultural divide these kids represent stems directly from the sustained experience they have had playing interactive Dragon Quest-like games. What this exposure has given them is a direct sense, not readily available in Japanese culture through other means, of playing multiple roles in the same context, of asking the "what if" questions they could never comfortably ask before (because of the Shinto superstition that saying a thing would make it happen), of making different complex trade-off decisions and then having the chance to observe contingent sets of outcomes, and—perhaps most important—of revisiting basic "rules of the game" and, when necessary, even reprogramming them.

The implicit message in all this, which is completely alien to traditional Japanese culture and education, is that it is possible to actively take control of one's situation or circumstances and, thereby, to change one's fate. Nothing need be accepted as an unalterable *fait accompli*. No one need submit passively to the dictates of external authority. Everything can be explored, rearranged, reprogrammed. Nothing has to be fixed or final. Everything, finally, is open to considered choice, initiative, creativity—and daring.

Consider, for example, the students at Keio University's experimental Fujisawa campus. Because they are all on-line, they can offer real-time reactions and contributions to the curriculum, to the structure of their own programs of study, to the content of their courses, and to the quality of their instructors. If they need information to supplement a text they are reading or a report they are writing, they can track it down through Internet. If they want to consult an expert anywhere in the world, they can reach him or her the same way. What a professor says in class no longer has to be treated as unquestioned gospel. If they have doubts, they can use the network to raise them and to solicit alternative points of view. They have stopped being passive consumers of an educational experience defined, shaped, and evaluated by the Ministry of Education. The technology has allowed them, in a most non-Japanese fashion, to become definers and shapers and evaluators—and questioners—themselves.

For the Japanese, this is an entirely new way of thinking. As such, it represents a deep rupture between generations, not something shared between them. It cuts, at last, the already thinly stretched cord, severing both the vertical linkages across age groups and the relationships of authority that have long held Japanese society together. In their place, it weaves new connections—not, however, with older cohorts of Japanese, but with the tens of millions of kids everywhere else in the world who have learned to play the same sorts of games and have so been exposed to the same implicit lessons. The web of culture used to be spun out of the stories a child heard at a grandparent's knee. In today's increasingly subnuclear families, it derives from a child's experience with interactive multimedia.

The social glue of intimate familiarity and shared experience once came only from participation in and with family. Now it comes from watching how a kid from another culture whom you've never seen before reveals character and mind-set through programming style. But it goes further, too. The kids in Japan amd elsewhere who master a joy stick-driven environment can move, with unbelievable speed, to comparable mastery of a PC's alphanumeric keyboard. This is especially important in Japan, where shared problems of writing and typing have long been a source of in-group social cohesion. Today, millions of Nintendo kids have ready access to multiple avenues of external communication. This is even truer for their younger siblings and will be truer still for their children. The link among generations has been broken; a new link with those sharing similar experiences has been forged.

THE "BRUTAL FILTER"

Reflecting on the huge waves of immigration from Europe that changed the demography of the United States during the 19th century, the historian Oscar Handlin described the upheaval triggered by such large-scale social movements as one of passing through a "brutal filter." Along the way, some—but not all—of the ties and allegiances snapped that had long kept the members of particular Old World societies bound together. Deeply entrenched connections between generations came unrooted. Inevitably, the elements and groupings so abruptly set free came together in the new country in countless new combinations and permutations—a true "melting pot" of possibilities. Some linkages entirely disappeared; some survived intact; some new ones were formed; all were changed.

Worldwide, the experience of today's Nintendo kids is leading evidence that the tastes, preferences, and even mind-sets of individuals around the world are beginning to move—if at different speeds and in different sequences—through an analogously brutal filter into the melting pot of the borderless economy. This late-20th-century wave of immigration and convergence is being driven, on the surface, by the development of global brands and popular culture and, at a much deeper level, by the infectious spread of new information-related technologies. It is a new kind of social process, something we have never seen before, and it is leading to a new kind of social reality: a genuinely cross-border civilization, nurtured by exposure to common technologies and sources of information, in which horizontal linkages within the same generation in different parts of the world are stronger than traditional, vertical linkages between generations in particular parts of it.

The journey is still at a fairly early stage. Even so, it is possible to see its broad contours and general direction. The countries from which these uprooted people are independently setting out are traditional, politically defined nation states. The country to which they are all migrating—helped along the way by shared exposure to the English language, to the Internet, to Fox TV, the BBC, CNN, and MTV, and by interactive communication tools—is the global economy of the borderless world.

Not surprisingly, national governments tend to resist, rather than encourage, such migration. For them, convergence is a problem, not a happy indication of positive forces at work. In resisting, their purpose is not so much to oppose California-ization itself or to frustrate their citizens' desire for the best and the cheapest products from around the world. Their concern, instead, is to protect the jobs of small, but politically powerful, special-interest groups. That is why they so often forbid or restrict imports (in the United States, steel and textiles), defend natural resources against foreign "exploiters" (Malaysia in the years before Prime Minister Mahathir's "Look East" program), or force their citizens to select from among either unduly expensive products (high-priced beef and rice in Japan) or high-priced and poor-quality products (automobiles in Australia, India, and Brazil). Over time, however, the explosive flow of information renders these tactics increasingly unworkable.

In the face of insistent, knowledgeable demand, nation states are less and less able to dictate individual economic choices. Should they try to do so in too restrictive a fashion, electronically based flows of capital will head elsewhere, penalizing their currencies and starving them of funds for investment. And individual transactions will migrate to channels that lie out of their sight as well as out of their reach.

Using a telephone, fax machine, or personal computer linked to the Internet, for example, a Japanese consumer in Sapporo can place an order for clothing with Lands' End in Wisconsin or L. L. Bean in Maine, have the merchandise delivered by UPS or Yamato, and charge the purchase to American Express, Visa, or MasterCard. That same consumer can also access software support or remote computer repair services provided, say, by a company based in Singapore or Kuala Lumpur but relying on Indian engineers based in Bombay and on database maintenance carried out in China. Moreover, even with Japan's tight control on banking activities, that same consumer can call or fax First Direct in Great Britain or any number of financial institutions in the United States 24 hours a day, transfer money from anywhere to anywhere, and so avoid the artificially low interest rates imposed by the government to protect domestic banks weakened by the collapse of the bubble economy.[7,8]

For Nintendo kids, this will be a normal part of everyday life. By end-running Japan's traditional business systems, they will save money, boost flexibility, and increase their range of choice. But they will also make an ever-larger share of their economic transactions effectively invisible to government. Where—in any of these business systems—can customs officers charge duties, local governments claim value-added taxes, or bureaucrats compile accurate trade statistics?

Thus, as more and more individuals pass through the brutal filter separating old-fashioned geographies from the global economy, power over economic activity will inevitably migrate from the central governments of nation states to the borderless network of countless individual, market-based decisions. In recent years, only where armed might has intervened, or threatened to intervene, in the name of "national interest" have governments been able to ignore with impunity—and then only at the cost of yet more harm to their people's quality of life—the corrosive effects on their political control of the natural flows of economic activity in a borderless economy.[9] And in the new melting pot of today's cross-border civilization, these flows will only gain in strength and depth.

Chapter Four

THE CIVIL MINIMUM

In a borderless economy, the workings of the market's "invisible hand" have a reach and a strength beyond anything that Adam Smith could have ever imagined. In Smith's day, economic activity took place on a landscape largely defined—and circumscribed—by the political borders of nation states: England with its wool, Portugal with its wines. Now, by contrast, it is economic activity that defines the landscape on which all other institutions, including the apparatus of statehood, must operate.

For John Maynard Keynes, that great prophet of modern economic thought, the laws that ultimately had to be obeyed were laws that defined the inescapable relationships between economic activities within a nation state. If demand increased, supply would follow. If supply increased, so would the number of jobs. If the economy needed stimulation, lower interest rates and heightened government spending would provide it. If the economy needed to be cooled down, higher interest rates would do it. In practice, of course, the devil would always be in the details, and the precise degree to turn this or that knob of policy might take some effort to determine. But, given sensible calculations and sophisticated modifications of theory, twisting that knob would lead to the outcomes desired. People might differ, of course, on just what those outcomes should be, but they were pretty much of a single mind—except for the extreme fringe of monetarist opinion—on how to get there. As President Nixon said, "We are all Keynesians now."

We are no longer. In a borderless economy, an increase in demand in one country may boost supply—and with it, the number of jobs—in another. Even if the new increment of supply were to be domestically provided, it might have a negligible effect on blue- or even white-collar employment, given the recent improvements in productivity made possible by computers and robots, or "steel-collar" workers.[1] Moreover, far from automatically raising supply at home, lower interest rates might just as easily drive supply-nurturing capital abroad to other countries where the promised returns look more attractive. And higher interest rates, far from depressing consumption-related demand, might actually ratchet it up—at least in the short run—by creating fear that resurgent inflation will only make things more expensive in the future.

On questions of economic policy, therefore, the tables have turned—with a vengeance. As the previous chapters have shown, the nation state has rapidly become an unnatural, even dysfunctional, unit in terms of which to think about or organize economic activity. This should occasion no real surprise. As the creation of a much earlier stage of industrial history, it has neither the will nor the incentive nor the credibility nor the tools nor the political base to play an effective role in a genuinely borderless economy.[2]

By heritage and by experience, nation states are comfortable with the market's invisible hand only when they control the far more visible robot arm to which it is attached. By virtue of their orientation and their skills, they cannot help but make economic choices primarily in terms of their political, not their economic, consequences. By the rules of electoral logic and popular expectation, they must always sacrifice general, indirect, long-term benefits in favor of immediate, tangible, and focused payoffs. They are a willing hostage to the past because the future is a constituency that casts no vote. No wonder they have grown out of place as actors in a global economy. Virtually by definition, they are unable to put global logic—that is, the true "quality of life" interests of all their people—first in any of the decisions they make.

GOVERNMENT PERFORMANCE

This marked inability to accept—or even acknowledge—global logic is slowly but surely dissolving the fabric holding nation states together. It used to be possible, for example, for governments to exercise monopoly control over the information their people received and, by doing so, to implicitly dictate their economic choices. In Japan, for example, before the Meiji Restoration, the monopoly was virtually complete: as a matter of policy, Japan had minimal contact with the outside world through an island known as Dejima in Nagasaki Prefecture. What information did come in from abroad was kept in libraries, to which only a handful of carefully selected scholars and bureaucrats had access. Common citizens did not. Even after the country "opened up" to the rest of the world in the 1850s, government remained the primary collection and distribution point for all cross-border information exchange.

As a result, the picture Japanese citizens received of developments elsewhere—who was strong militarily, who posed an economic threat—was entirely the product of government decision. As, of course, were the media reports, school textbooks, and forms of training that the government either provided itself or approved. So, too, for that matter, was information about the situation at home. Were food and fuel supplies so very limited that an expansionist effort to dominate other geographical areas was necessary? Only the government really knew. And, to their great cost, the people only knew what the government chose to tell them.

Happily, because Japan today is an active part of the borderless economy, its government cannot monopolize information so completely. By contrast, North Korea and Myanmar are not, and their governments can—and do. Deng Xiaoping's famous parable of birds in the cage is a good case in point: leaders are afraid of letting them out for fear they will never come back. Quite rightly, these governments see control of information as a critical part of their apparatus of political control, and they have been willing to pay—or, rather, to have their citizens pay—the price for it in a grossly diminished standard of living. These regimes understand all too well that a free flow of accurate information about conditions at home or quality of life elsewhere would bring their people into the streets and their dictatorship to its knees. Unlike more open environments, where an enhanced flow of information helps make government control stable by speeding—and smoothing—the transition to a genuine market economy, in countries like these it can nurture a market only by rudely bursting the shackles of control.

Japan maintained its self-willed isolation long before the appearance of modern information technology; North Korea and Myanmar do so afterwards. To enable a meaningful flow of information, such technology is a necessary, but not a sufficient, condition. Something else is needed: a certain readiness or receptivity on the part of individuals, whether in their role as citizens or as consumers. As the history of developing economies in Asia and elsewhere indicates, when GNP per capita reaches something like the $5,000 level, discretionary income crosses an invisible threshold. Above it, there is enough margin in economic life for people to begin wondering whether they have reasonable access to the best and cheapest available products and services and whether they have an adequate quality of life. More troubling for those in political control, people also begin to wonder whether their government is doing as well by them as it might. Global flows of information discipline the governments of nation states.

In Taiwan, which has crossed that threshold, people have begun to look critically at their own lifestyles and at the economic opportunities around them, and to question the politicians' insistence on remaining in a perpetual state of war with the mainland.[3] Similarly, in South Korea, there was such popular pressure to relax travel restrictions (so honeymooners and others could enjoy in person the lovely areas of Hawaii and Australia that they had often seen on television) that tourism was finally deregulated in 1991. There was even pressure to stop blaming Japan for all the problems at home.

For a half century and more, the South Korean government has taught its people that the Japanese are merciless imperialists who may work hard but who have ice where their hearts should be. When travel restrictions were relaxed in the early 1990s, floods of Korean honeymooners made their way to Kyushu, a southwestern island in Japan sprinkled with volcanoes, hot springs, and lovely flowers. Once there, they discovered that the Japanese are, in fact, quite human, quite capable of smiling and being gracious to visitors, and—in many ways—quite like Koreans themselves. This has made it increasingly difficult for the Korean government to lay at Japan's door plausible blame for everything that does not go well at home. For growing numbers of Koreans, such demonizing of Japan and the Japanese simply does not square with their own personal experience of the country and its people.

As a result, it has become much easier to acknowledge that many of South Korea's problems with the deregulation and globalization of its economy stem directly from the intense, parochial nationalism so painstakingly crafted and maintained by President Kim Yong Sam's predecessors. Indeed, as one high-ranking trade official in Seoul told me recently, "The reason we have proposed that Korea provide the chairmanship for the new World Trade Organization is that we may not be able to leapfrog to an open economy on our own. But if the WTO had a Korean chairman, our strongly nationalistic people will not let him down. So it will be much easier for them to support measures to deregulate and open up our economy."

The exact details will vary from country to country, but the general pattern is clear: with subsistence ensured, discretionary money available, and information about the rest of the world accessible, people will inevitably start to look around them and ask why they cannot have what others have. Equally important, they will start to ask why they were not able to have it in the past. They will also look with a much more critical eye at the performance of their government in general as a coordinator of individual access to the good things in life.

Such a performance review is not likely to be pleasant. When governments control information—and, in large measure, because they do—it is all too easy for them to believe that they "own" the people. That usually means restricting access to certain kinds of goods or services or pricing them far above what economic logic would dictate.

If the market-driven level of consumption conflicts with some pet government policy or with its general desire for control, as it often does, the obvious response is to restrict consumption. And if people would choose otherwise if given the opportunity, so what? Don't give it to them. Don't even let them know you're not going to do so. What they don't know can't hurt you—or, much of the time, your favored allies and confederates, those interest groups that, one way or another, do so much to prop up your regime.

In Singapore recently, the government aggressively questioned a newspaper for what it found a most disturbing bit of "illegal" activity: making public government data on the country's economic growth rate. This kind of official attitude, if sustained over time and applied to a broad range of information, will certainly cause that economy—and any market economy—to stagnate. The reason is simple: in market-based societies, it is the free flow of information that fuels the economic engine. Cut it off or cut it back and you starve that engine of what it most needs to operate. Still, the temptation to close the valve at least part of the way is often hard to resist. Indeed, above the $5,000 threshold, when performance questions start to get asked it is not just political leaders, but the whole network of cronies, middle-men, and bureaucrats whose attachments to—and benefits from—the established system come under threat.

NATION STATES AND THEIR DISCONTENTS

Experience teaches that governments usually respond in one of three ways to such a threat. If the information monopoly is still fairly solid and connections with the borderless economy are not essential, they may face it down with force or the threat of force. This, of course, is the black hole into which outlaw regimes so easily fall. If the monopoly is incomplete but still powerful and the pressures for change uncoordinated, they may try to tough it out. But if the monopoly is leaky and public pressure substantial, they may try to buy it off.

In the more developed economies, this third option is usually the response of choice. And for a while, though incredibly expensive, it usually works. The only problem is that, over time, it probably does more than either of the other responses to eat away at the fabric of the nation state that adopts it. Neither rattling sabers nor inserting earplugs threatens the existence of the state. They may well provoke sufficient hostility to overthrow individual leaders or whole governments, but they do not usually lead to an erosion of the nation state itself. The third option does.

Faced with rising demands from an ever-more complex mix of domestic constituencies, governments following this third option climb, in effect, not so gently onto the back of a very moody tiger. They cannot safely get off. Once it becomes known that they are willing to respond to the many claimants to their resources by buying them off as cheaply as possible, the number of claimants lining up for their turn inevitably skyrockets. As does the level of support that satisfies.

Worse, as public expectations about the legitimacy of such support harden, it becomes progressively more difficult for governments to revoke the principle or to exclude, as a matter of either policy or discretionary judgment, any but the most marginal categories of people with outstretched hands. Worse still, once the entitlement mentality gets so fully entrenched that demands on the nation's resources exceed the available supply, the reaction of interested constituencies is not to adopt a more moderate stance or to offer to accept less in the name of the common good. It is, rather, to turn with a vengeance on competing constituencies in hopes of discrediting them or otherwise capturing part of their share. And it is precisely this kind of intramural skirmishing that produces the acid most likely to eat away the fabric of the nation state.

In practice, here's how the process usually works. Japan, for example, has a few urban areas with great population density, as well as many outlying regions and islands that are much more sparsely settled. In the name of fairness to its multiple claimants and as a way of showing that its monopoly of power is equitable, the government agrees to provide a common level of public services everywhere in the country. This "civil minimum"—in phone service, for example—applies whether you live on the remote island of Okinawa or in the heart of downtown Tokyo. Much the same is true of postal service, water supply, electrical power, and a host of other government-funded services.

The problem, of course, is that the cost of providing these services varies wildly among regions, and some inevitably wind up subsidizing—or believing that they are subsidizing—others. Worse, citizens in the more remote locations start to expect, and then to demand, the same level of service from the central government—the same railroads and schools and harbors and highways—enjoyed by those closer to the center. These pressures, in turn, force local politicians to metamorphose from disinterested public servants into lobbyists and "pork-bearers" for their own little towns or districts. No longer can they afford to keep their attention focused on the greater public good or on broad questions about the budget deficit or global economic trends. Rising expectations at home have redefined their role: they are now, first and foremost, merchants of pork.[4]

If the economy is healthy, the quality of life improving, and the tax burden on individuals felt to be relatively light, such subsidies usually pass without notice. But when the economic picture is less rosy or when increased information about lifestyles elsewhere boosts expectations too rapidly, envy and resentment begin to spread. Do I, as a hardworking middle manager in a Tokyo-based corporation, as someone who lives in a small apartment and has to spend more than three hours a day commuting to and from work on crowded trains, really not begrudge the money spent on efficient services for rural farmers in Tohoku district? Not likely—especially if the images brought to my home television screen show me the extremely attractive way my peers live even in countries like Italy or Australia, where the GNP per capita is less than half that of Japan. And especially if I feel that the good life that my hard work buys for me and my family lags far behind the contribution that my efforts make to the nation's economic performance.

If the expense of urban housing means that I have to commute 40 or 50 kilometers to my job in Tokyo in trains packed like sardine cans, much of the countryside I can see out the window is covered with small farms and rice paddies. In fact, within a 50-kilometer radius of Tokyo, 65 percent of the land—nearly 330,000 hectares of some of the most expensive property in the world—is devoted to wildly inefficient agriculture. If only one quarter of this land were sold for private housing, Tokyo-area families would be able to afford 120 to 150 square meters of living space, instead of today's average of 88 square meters (Exhibit 4–1). Moreover, cheaper—and more available—land would cut the cost of essential public works like providing better sewage, removing traffic bottlenecks, and double-tracking commuter trains.

Why is this not possible now? There are three reasons—all nation state-based and all irrelevant. First, because it feels it must be fair and evenhanded in its treatment of all farmers and fishermen across the

EXHIBIT 4–1

Housing: Size and Price

	Floor space m²	Price $ Thousands
Australia (1993)	191.0	96.6
U.S.A. (1992)	153.2	121.0
South Korea (1993)	119.3	N.A.
U.K. (1992)	95.0	104.4
Germany (1993)	90.8	134.0
Japan (1993)	88.6	372.6

Sources: U.S. Bureau of the Census; National Association of Realtors data for U.S.A. 1992; Nationwide Building Society data for U.K.; Federal Statistical Office data for Germany; Bank of Korea; Construction Association of Korea data for Korea; Australian Bureau of Statistics; Real Estate Institute of Australia for Australia.

country, the Ministry of Agriculture and Fisheries (MOAF) does not want to apply different criteria to different regions. There can, then, be no exception made for Tokyo. If people in other parts of the country grow rice and catch fish, so should—and will—those in the greater Tokyo region. If the land allocated to rice farming shrinks over time as domestic rice consumption falls, the shrinkage around Tokyo can be no more and no less than the shrinkage elsewhere. Fair is fair.

Second, as an institution, MOAF does not want to see the amount of farming in the Tokyo metropolitan area fall very much, because the bureaucrats who run it have no desire to lose their status, disrupt their lives, and move away from Tokyo. Administrative reform efforts within the government have created substantial pressure to relocate nonessential bureaus and activities to less expensive areas outside Tokyo. MOAF has no interest in volunteering. But it does have an interest in keeping plenty of vocal farmers in the Tokyo area, and keeping them active on its behalf.

And third, although Japan has only 170,000 full-time and 4,300,000 part-time farmers, whose income from farming, on average, now represents less than 20 percent of their total household income, there are some 420,000 clerks in the various farmers cooperatives, who handle all the paperwork related to agricultural products, fertilizers, pesticides, and the the like. And, of course, there are the 90,000 bureaucrats in MOAF, of whom as many as 11,000 spend their time classifying different grades of rice. So in debates over land use and in trade negotiations with the United States, it is abundantly clear where the ministry's interest—as well as that of its allies—lies. However, the interest of the Japanese people, *and even of Japanese farmers,* lies somewhere else.

Japanese consumers have, at last, begun to figure this out. Increasingly, the civil minimum no longer appeals to them as a fair enough economic "glue" to hold the body politic together. It seems more like exploitation. If I am a hardworking middle manager, I resent it, and I resent the government that provides it. For years, given the nature of its political base, the Liberal Democratic Party (LDP) was markedly reluctant to change the comparative electoral weight of votes from rural, traditional farming areas and from urban or suburban areas, whose residents are largely driving the country's dynamic economic growth. In terms of political influence, the former now count four times more than the latter. As a salaryman and consumer, I see no sense in this. After all, what have the farmers or fishermen done for me recently? Why should I have to pay the excessive cost of the food that we could just as easily—and much more cheaply—import from abroad?

The government tells me, Remember how much hunger there was throughout the country during World War II and in the years immediately after it? That must never happen again. And so we must pay any price and absorb any political inefficiency or apparent unfairness in order to make ourselves self-sufficient in food. But the government's logic simply does not hold water. I know it. Everybody knows it. Our country is totally dependent on imported food and fuel anyway. We have oil reserves that will last, at most, for 180 days. If there is an emergency, just what is it that we are supposed to cook our rice with on the 181st day that we have given up our votes to obtain? Many other necessary daily commodities will be exhausted long before we get to the bottom of our rice mountain. Who is fooling whom?[5]

The answer to many of these questions became clear in 1993 when Japan suffered an unusually cold summer growing season and its rice crop fell 30 percent short. The emergency reserve that MOAF was supposed to have saved up—all 180 days of it—was not there. In panic, the government made the uncomfortable public decision to import some 300,000 tons. It then made a far more comfortable private decision to sell that imported rice at inflated domestic rates, to keep the difference between those rates and international prices—more than US $1 billion—entirely for itself, and to use it to further subsidize domestic farmers, who were politically unhappy with the decision to import. Regular consumers enjoyed none of the benefit. The farmers, moreover, also received—and kept—ample insurance payments for their damaged crops. Thus, their income was much higher in the disastrous conditions of 1993 than in 1994, when the crop was unusually good. And MOAF's influence—notwithstanding the abject failure of its contingency measures—was greater. This is perverse.

Still, it has been very difficult in Japan, which is such a small country, to convince people that having one system, one civil minimum, is bad policy. The reality, of course, is that because Japan's different regions have developed in very different ways, the distribution in the ratio of what regions contribute to what they receive is dramatically uneven, despite the relatively flat distribution of wealth. Of the country's 47 prefectures, 44 are net recipients of government subsidies. The other three—Tokyo, Osaka, and Aichi (Nagoya)—pay for the rest. The imbalance is striking. More than 85 percent of Japan's wealth is created in the regions of Tokyo, Osaka, Fukuoka, Sapporo, and Nagoya. All the others receive more from the central government than they pay in.

This arrangement is both reflected in and sustained by the country's voting patterns. The heart of the LDP's traditional support came from the rural areas, to which it returned a disproportionate share of the centrally provided subsidies, in the form either of direct grants of money or services (such as for the construction of highways, railroads, harbors, airports, and dams) or of indirect protection like trade barriers against the import of foreign rice or beef. LDP stands for Liberal Democratic Party, but what it practiced for years is nothing but rural socialism. Similarly, the Japan Socialist Party (JSP) has been practicing labor socialism. Together, they have devoted all their energies to redistributing wealth, in vote-conscious ways, so as to subsidize the poorly managed regions and uncompetitive industries that keep them in power.

If I live in one of Japan's three major cities, this arrangement quickly begins to lose its appeal. I may be as reasonable as the next man, but it is hard to see why I should keep footing this kind of bill. Give me access to land, give me access to the good life, give me a ballot that counts every bit as much as the next man's. That's what I want—not a huge tax that goes to support farmers or some other fringe constituency. Taking money out of my pocket to support such groups is acceptable for a while in the name of fairness. But how long is "a while?" The logic of doing this forever is hard for me to grasp. Force that policy on me without explanation, ignore my concerns, and ratchet up the unequal contribution I already have to make, and I will start to question the whole system. In political terms, the road from "let's be a bit more equitable in sharing the burden" to "who needs those fringe groups anyway?" is painfully short.

For their part, of course, these groups think they get, if anything, too little. After all, their need is greater and the difficulties of their lives more pronounced. Why should they be treated as second-class citizens? Either they are a part of Japan or not. If they are, then there is no legitimate reason why they should watch the civil minimum being applied elsewhere but not at home, particularly with respect to lifestyle issues.[6]

In the good old days, individual Japanese citizens would never have complained. They were taught and trained not to object to what the government said or did, but to accept it without a murmur. Today, however, the marked disparity in economic burden, coupled with an equally marked disparity in lifestyle, has finally begun to tear up that old social fabric and, with it, that old habit of acquiescence. This may sound like an exaggeration but it is not. At long last, the Japanese are finally joining the rest of informed industrial society.

Throughout the Triad, this predictable cycle of political emotion and its symmetrical dynamic of envy and resentment have become regular features of the political landscape. Once governments embark on a policy geared to the civil minimum, to protectionism for special interests, they tend to stay with it no matter what, and, where possible, to throw additional benefits in the way of those who complain the loudest. This is because the concrete, visible dangers of even trying to climb off this particular tiger are too frightening to contemplate.

The problem is that the dangers of staying aboard, though less immediately tangible and far harder to see, are often much greater. Trying to climb off puts only the current government and its leaders at risk;

trying to stay aboard ultimately threatens the nation state itself. Historically, the ethos of equally shared *contributions* to the common good (even though the benefits may not be shared quite so equally) has been the foundation on which genuinely democratic societies, no less than the nations that grow up around them, rest. When that ethos wanes or goes into eclipse, so does the glue that holds those nations together. The tyranny of modern democracy is that it tends to give equal weight to votes *before* contributions to the maintenance of society as a whole are taken into account. Everywhere, the result is the same: elected officials, just like the candidates trying to replace them, focus their attention and their language on a promised equality of results, not of contribution.

To be sure, some governments, though politically unable to back away from their commitment to the civil minimum or to the protection of domestic industries no matter how weak they are, have begun to experiment with other means to the same end. In the United States, for example, the great upsurge in industry deregulation during the 1970s and 1980s had the effect of letting the allocation of many services—local availability of air transport for one—be set by market forces. Much the same is true of other countries that have begun to experiment with serious programs of privatization and other forms of market liberalization, including deregulation.[7]

These developments have, indeed, trimmed away some of the more obvious domestic cross-subsidies, but they have done so only imperfectly. In the United States, deregulation of the airline industry was not accompanied by deregulation of airport gates or landing slots, which meant a stronger, not a weaker, oligopoly. Moreover, the political price for deregulation has often been a renewed government commitment to a threshold or "safety net" level of service (a basic level of telephone service in the United States, for example) that remains available to all—and remains funded out of general revenues. In Japan, the privatization of NTT has led to a much stronger Ministry of Communications and Postal Services (MOCPOS), which now has life-and-death power over NTT, as well as over the newly introduced common carriers, through its control of pricing and other approval processes.

Before NTT was privatized it was a prominent state-owned enterprise, a powerful bureaucracy that reported to no one. After its "libera-tion" from nominal state control with the partial sale of its shares to the public in February of 1987, its largest shareholder—at least tech-nically—became the Ministry of Finance. Moreover, as a private com-pany, NTT now has to get approval for changes in tariffs or for new services from MOCPOS. Today, the company has to file all its pricing strategies for distance, time, and type of call—some 12,000 different items in all—with MOCPOS. Worse, MOCPOS now wants to break up NTT—a US $60 billion enterprise with 250,000 employees—into nine regional companies. Lawmakers are sympathetic. Nine baby-NTTs means nine regional headquarters to regulate and preside over, and nine management staffs on which MOCPOS officials can find po-sitions after they reach the mandatory retirement age of 55. This is not exactly what Prime Minister Yasuhiro Nakasone's powerful administra-tive reform group had in mind when it moved in 1985 to free NTT from government bureaucracy.

This kind of situation, whether in Japan or elsewhere in the Triad, has become painfully familiar. Wherever it occurs, it leads to political gridlock. No sitting government has been willing or able to climb off the civil minimum tiger or resist the pressure from special interests. Even worse, the government consistently tightens not only its hold on the tiger's back, but also its own centralized power, by its ability to raise and distribute taxpayers' money. The more the economic positions of the rich, the poor, and the geographical regions are determined by the artifice of government-defined policies and government-defined distri-butions, the less the whole arrangement squares with the logic of either economics or equity.

What began as a system to serve, fairly, the interests of the people in-exorably becomes little more than a system to conserve centralized power. And when, as inevitably happens, that power is threatened by more demands than it can reasonably meet—when the tiger proves too hungry—the power turns to the presses and prints more money. To stay comfortably in the saddle today, it will shamelessly mortgage the future. This, of course, is not the way to promote healthy growth. All it does is redistribute inequalities. Like the United States,[8] Canada,[9] and many European countries, Japan has funded these obligations by issu-ing so many long-term (30-year) bonds that it has virtually exhausted its capacity to borrow against the earning power of its children. Accordingly, the government has now proposed funding its ambitious plans for an information superhighway by issuing 60-year bonds—that is, by mortgaging the earning power of its grandchildren.

In all industrialized countries, the price of staying aboard and staying generous has been an ever larger and increasingly inefficient allocation of resources. In the past, these subsidies were never supportive of overall levels of competitiveness; at best, the burden they added was not large enough to trouble otherwise healthy economies. Today, even that is changing. Because many of the Triad economies are struggling, the absolute burden imposed by these civil minimums and interest-group subsidies is a quite real—and visible—problem.

Adding to these burdens, of course, is the steadily growing share of the civil minimum demanded of government in the form of broad-based social programs—welfare, unemployment compensation, public education, old-age pensions, health insurance, and the like. Beyond the sheer financial difficulties these social payments cause, they reflect an even more troubling schizophrenia in the public mind. As recent elections in almost all the industrial democracies make clear, vocal and influential constituencies of citizens do not want these benefits reduced but, as taxpayers, they do not want to pay for them. The inevitable result: on the provider side, an illogical patchwork of support that ratchets ever upward; and, perhaps more troubling, on the receiving side, an ever-greater addiction to such support. It is hard, indeed, to think of an industry or a region that, once hooked on the civil minimum, has returned to freestanding health.

In Germany, for example, the costs of these programs already add up to roughly 33 percent of GDP. By the year 2030, if present trends continue, they will account for nearly 50 percent. This would precipitate a fiscal disaster. If Germany chose to pay for these services by issuing bonds, the interest payments would be crushing. If it chose to pay for them through taxation, the confiscatory rates would either drive competitive businesses elsewhere or lead them to substitute more capital (in the form of additional machines and automation) for people. This, of course, would lift unemployment yet another notch and so boost still further the social costs requiring heightened taxation in the first place.

However they get funded, social benefits and costs of this magnitude inevitably reduce the motivation of people to work at their current jobs, to make that current work more productive, and even—when necessary—to accept alternative employment at lower wages. Again, in Germany, the average manufacturing worker's annual days off for vacation, public holiday, and sick leave (but not counting days lost through strikes or maternity leave) come to 61—more than double the number in the United States or Japan.[10] In total, all the nonwage labor costs associated with such workers add up to half the total cost of manpower. Inevitably, competitiveness suffers.

But there is worse, much worse. The cycles of envy and resentment to which these arrangements inevitably lead have grown steadily more pronounced. In many countries, Japan included, they have become troublesome enough to have engendered serious public disaffection with the whole gridlocked system of which they are a key part. By all relevant measures, governments are flunking, badly flunking, the performance test. At the same time, these cycles have steadily eaten away at the communalist ethos that has traditionally held these nations together. And all this, remember, is happening at a time when the major flows of economic activity in a borderless world no longer follow the channels marked out by the boundary lines on political maps.

The unhappy fact is that, in most modern nations, the government has strangely—but all too understandably—become an enemy of the public at large. The bulk of the working population, the so-called "silent majority" that for years provided a stable center of social and political gravity, no longer has access to parties that truly represent its communal interests. Instead, established political systems have more and more become the creature of special interests and the poorer geographical districts, which regularly trade their support for its protection and largesse. Tokyo, for example, has produced only one prime minister (Ichiro Hatoyama) during the past 50 years. Among former prime ministers, Noboru Takeshita comes from the very poorest prefecture, Shimane; Tsutomi Hata from Nagano, the "Alps" of Japan; and Morihiro Hosokawa from the island of Kyushu (as, for that matter, does the current incumbent, Tomiichi Murayama). The "shadow shogun," Shin Kanemaru, came from the smallest prefecture, Yamanashi; the powerful Ichiro Ozawa, from the "Tibet" of Japan, Iwate prefecture.

This growing alignment of government power with domestic special interests and have-not regions makes it virtually impossible for those at the center to adopt responsible policies for a nation as a whole, let alone for its participation in the wider borderless economy—and this at a time when prosperity at home is increasingly the result of support from abroad. It does not seem to matter that, as recent analyses by the World Bank have demonstrated yet again, free trade and a free flow of economic activity work, on balance, to raise everyone's standard of living. The alignments of power pay little, if any, heed to such sentiments. They represent only themselves, not the people or the people's interests.

No matter how understandable the political or even social pressures behind these alignments, they make no sense economically. Investing money inefficiently never does. In a borderless world, where economic interdependence creates ever-higher degrees of sensitivity to other economies,[11] it is inherently unsustainable. Sooner or later, usually sooner, the invisible hand of the market will move value-creating activity elsewhere. During the past several years, for instance, the Japanese government has pumped more than US $300 billion into the domestic economy in a Keynesian attempt to jump-start demand and so create new jobs in the wake of the post-bubble recession. The plan worked. Demand did increase. Jobs too. But the new increments of supply came from—and new jobs were created in—China, Korea, and the rest of the world, not Japan. In other words, what the United States experienced in the '80s Japan is going through now, with far greater difficulty and agony.

The inevitable result of prolonged detachment from the public at large is a further erosion both of trust in government and of the traditional nation state as a significant unit of economic activity. As a practical matter, given its long experience on the back of the tiger, no central government will find it easy to redress—or even rethink—the imbalance among its constituent regions. What seems fair to some will seem extremely unfair to others. The pieces cannot be put together again.

Chapter Five

"NATIONAL INTEREST"
AS A DECLINING INDUSTRY

But why, it is reasonable to ask, does the glue that held traditional nation states together no longer seem to work? Why can the pieces not be put together again? Are our leaders going about a perfectly doable task, but in a wrong and badly outdated way? Or is it that the task itself has become impossible to accomplish?

The intense burst of "throw the rascals out" sentiment, which so boldly colored recent elections in France, Italy, Japan, the United States, and other parts of the industrialized world, points toward an answer. Certainly it reflects, in part, widespread disgust with the feverish and often corrupt attempts of those in power to stay there. As one columnist aptly noted, "The less the old parties have to offer the electorate, the more desperate they are to raise the campaign funds to stay in power; the more spent they are as a historical force, the more they need to spend."[1] But it also reflects a deeper sense that more is going on than just an excessive level of abuse of an otherwise workable political system.

There is growing sentiment that that system itself—the much patched and mended apparatus of the modern nation state—is an inadequate mechanism for dealing with the threats and opportunities of a global economy. Indeed, according to Gianni De Michelis, the former foreign minister of Italy, "We are witnessing the explosion of a long-obsolete model of liberal democracy that can no longer accommodate our dynamic, complex societies with their sophisticated electorates of vast diversity and highly differentiated interest."

When the well-being of these societies depended on their safe and sure ability to exploit scarce natural resources, national interest was clear: protect those resources, with military force if necessary, and control their use. But as I have argued in *The Borderless World*[2] and elsewhere,[3] in today's knowledge-driven economy, the nations that still define their interests primarily in these terms—such as Brazil, Indonesia,[4] or Australia, and the oil-producing countries of the Middle East—suffer from what I call the "resource illusion."[5] In the name of protecting their national interest, they wall themselves off from the most powerful engines of growth.

Australia is a very good case in point. It has a land mass 20 times the size of Japan and fewer than 20 million people, more than 85 percent of whom live in major cities like Sydney, Melbourne, Adelaide, Brisbane, and Perth. Thus, despite the country's reputation as a commodity supplier of metals, minerals, and agricultural products, it is, in fact, quite an urban, knowledge-intensive society. Paul Keating, its prime minister, has made public his intention to take Australia out of the British Commonwealth and make it a freestanding republic by the year 2000—a republic, moreover, linked intimately with the other rapidly growing economies in Asia.

In comparison with those economies, Australia is perhaps the furthest along in applying computers and telecommunications to business and in developing amenity/lifestyle-oriented products and services—housing, furniture, interior design, landscaping, and environmental engineering, for example—at a reasonable cost.[6] These are the kinds of skills and products that will be in increasing demand as consumers in the rest of Asia focus ever more attention on their quality of life. Even so, Australian managers still tend to suffer from Asiaphobia. Japan, for example, could easily become Australia's biggest market for amenity-based products, but Australian housing projects still focus on Indonesia and engineering projects on Laos and Cambodia. Japan also accounts for more than 50 percent of its minerals exports, but none of the top executives from the relevant companies has ever lived in Japan. None speaks Japanese. Instead, these companies tend to rely for their Japan "presence" on Japanese trading firms.[7,8]

In fact, according to Peter Hartcher in the *Australian Financial Review*, "If Paul Keating were to invite Australia's three biggest exporters to a confidential briefing on Australian trade policy, he might be embarrassed to find that two of them are not Australian at all. After BHP, the next biggest exporters are Japanese trading houses . . . Mitsui and Mitsubishi . . . Alternatively, Keating might like to host a reception when he arrives in Tokyo in a couple of weeks for the Japan representatives of Australia's biggest 100 companies. It wouldn't need to be a lavish affair. He could hold it in a microbus. That's because only 14 of them have a representative in Japan, which only happens to be Australia's biggest market and the world's second-biggest economy."[9]

This is too sad to be funny. Less amusing still is the way foreign investment in Australia is restricted. The Foreign Investment Review Board (FIRB) issues guidelines on the upper limit of foreign ownership of Australian companies and on the ownership of real property. Equity participation over 15 percent requires special FIRB approval, which has traditionally gone (in descending order of preference) to companies from New Zealand, Britain, and the United States—an order hardly consistent with the prime minister's "Look North" policy. Moreover, if a foreigner buys a piece of land in Australia to build an apartment complex, he or she must start building on the land within one year, sell units off-the-plan (that is, before construction is completed), and ensure that at least 50 percent of the units get sold to Australian nationals.

State governments, such as those in Queensland and Victoria, tend to be a bit more flexible, but the central government still has its defenses up. The predictable result: not only low penetration of Asian markets, but also low investment in Australia, which has led, in turn, to spotty returns, a chronic—albeit entirely unnecessary—capital shortage, and a degree of volatility that discourages investment in the future. This is neither a sensible nor a sustainable strategy. If a country like Australia keeps the global economy at arm's length, its resources will, over time, become commodities, and commodity prices inevitably fall.

Growth depends on inviting the global economy in, not keeping it out. It depends on creating and leveraging value-adding economic linkages that ignore political borders, not on ruthlessly stamping them out in the name of "national interest" as an insult to the prerogatives of sovereignty. A closed-country model makes cities and regions rivals with each other. This is because the cities and regions—for example, Sydney and Melbourne or Osaka and Tokyo—feel that they are competing for a larger share of a finite-sized pie. The nation state solution assumes a "zero-sum" game for limited resources. The region state model, open to the global economy, is "plus sum" as prosperity is brought in from without.

More and more, however, "national interest" gets used as a knee-jerk defense of special interests, not of a people's interests. Consider, for a moment, the whaling industry in Japan. Today, there are only four companies with 500 or so people—total—devoted to whale hunting in the entire country. The reality is that not that many people eat whale meat or use whale oil anymore. As a result, even these companies have, for a long time, been diversifying into other areas.

But the whalers—and the bureaucrats in MOAF who nominally supervise them—are reluctant to sacrifice any of their influence or the economic benefits that flow from it. So they play, shamelessly but with a straight face, to national pride. Arrogant foreigners are telling us to stop, they complain. We shouldn't give in to that sort of ham-handed pressure; our national pride is at stake. Worse, those foreigners are being thoroughly hypocritical. In years past, they themselves were by far the most aggressive whalers in the world. Merely because they chose to stop, why should we?

This is, of course, transparent nonsense, but it is effective. Waving the flag usually is. If patriotism is, as Dr. Johnson used to remark, the last refuge of the scoundrel, wrapping outdated industry in the mantle of national interest is the last refuge of the economically dispossessed. In economic terms, pleading national interest is the declining cottage industry of those who have been bypassed by the global economy.

In their more responsible moments, those who work in this industry, as well as those who are swayed by its vocal protests, know better. They know they are fighting a losing, rearguard action. It is—and, at heart, they know that it is—an action that deserves to be lost. Its underlying cause may be perfectly understandable and its emotion genuine. The reason it affects policy, however, has nothing to do with comprehensibility or genuineness or competitiveness. In Japan and elsewhere, the maunderings of this cottage industry have the effect they do only because of the disproportionate political clout of the economically backward constituencies from which they come. Period.

Declining industries usually follow their own vicious cycle down. The competent players have all left, and those that remain are, as the Japanese proverb has it, trying to hang on to a straw as they drown. Few use their brains. Whale killing may be a declining industy, for example, but in Hawaii and elsewhere *whale-watching* has become quite an attractive—and lucrative—activity. Glasgow may have high unemployment and an out-of-the-way location, but it also offers an eager, low-cost source of labor and a convenient entry point to Europe for U.S. investment. A Japanese fishing port like Hachinohe may have fallen on hard times because youngsters no longer want to work in the rough seas off Okhotsk and the Russians are getting testy about enforcing their 200-mile exclusion zone. But Russian fishermen would be willing to sell their catches at appealing prices in exchange for access both to Japan's extensive market and to hard currency.

Moreover, if government subsidies to the Japanese fleet, which in the past have funded underutilized ships with elaborate electronics and refrigeration facilities, were also extended to the Russians, Japan's supply of fresh, northern fish—so essential to meeting domestic consumers' demand for sushi and sashimi—could be greatly expanded at relatively low cost. Alternatively, the Japanese could just loan the Russians their boats. Either way, everyone would benefit. "National interest," however, makes these arrangements unlikely: governments find it hard to justify spending money on anything that is not explicitly "theirs"—even when, in practice, the alternative is to pay out even more money, inefficiently, by way of subsidy.

Indeed, through the civil minimum, government typically responds to the backward-looking demands of hard-pressed industries by providing subsidies. Through trade, capital market, and regulatory policy, it responds to them by providing protection. Together, subsidies and protection neither create incentives for healthy, if deliberately paced, change, nor work to build a constituency in favor of such incentives.

The only thing they do is buy off current political opposition, and they do so at a horrendous cost—in money, lost employment, and potential for future growth—that must be absorbed by all citizens in their roles as workers and consumers. In fact, as a recent study by my former colleagues at McKinsey & Co. indicates quite clearly, government protection of domestic product markets is every bit as important a cause (if not more so) of escalating unemployment levels in all parts of the Triad[10] as rigidities in labor markets themselves.

My point is simple: in a borderless world, traditional national interest—which has become little more than a cloak for subsidy and protection—has no meaningful place. It has turned into a flag of convenience for those who, having been left behind, want not so much a chance to move forward as to hold others back as well. Let me repeat: this is a point about what usually goes wrong when economic activities and interest groups are bundled together in a single nation state, not about the value of co-locating such activities in the same geographical area. This distinction matters.

Several contemporary scholars—Michael Porter, in *The Competitive Advantage of Nations,*[11] being chief among them—have argued persuasively and, I think, correctly for the critical importance, especially in a global economy, of having clusters of related factor endowments located close together. Even in an information-driven age, skilled workers, extensive networks of supplier industries, and so on—the ingredients of what Porter calls the "diamond" of competitiveness—do, indeed, perform better when they exist in close geographical proximity. No argument here. It does not follow, however, that to be effective, such geographical groupings must co-exist within the borders of a single nation state, and thereby participate in the same national interest. Indeed, as I hope to show in the chapters to come, these necessary groupings work equally well—and perhaps even better—when they lie across political borders and so are free of the burden of national interest. Conversely, as Annalee Saxenian so clearly demonstrates in her book *Regional Advantage,*[12] Silicon Valley prospers but Boston's Route 128 declines, even though they are in the same country. At a minimum, the success of an industry or a region is not the function of a nation *per se,* but of the particular combination of individuals, institutions, and culture in this industry or that region.

This point is worth further attention. Studies of an industry's international competitiveness often overlook the entire spectrum of industry in the country in question. When, for instance, scholars around the world began to seek for explanations for Japan's great industrial success during the 1970s and 1980s, they quickly fastened on such explanations as the role of the Ministry of International Trade and Industry (MITI), the effectiveness of total quality management programs, the leverage provided by a zero-defects approach to manufacturing, and even the inscrutable camaraderie provided by company songs. Individually, each of these explanations—and many others like them—has some merit. Together, however, they add up to nothing. As I have repeatedly argued over the years,[13] it was not Japan that was so stunningly competitive, but only a handful of industries within Japan[14] and, more to the point, only a handful of companies led by strong individuals within those industries.[15]

Japan is the rule here, not the exception. Competitiveness does not flourish across the board. In Switzerland, there is world-class competitiveness only in the insurance, pharmaceutical, food, and machinery industries; in Germany, in the chemical and automotive industries; in Britain, in media-related businesses; in Australia, in mining and agricultural products; in the Philippines, in accounting services and brewing; in Sweden, in paper containers and power generation. During the 1980s in Japan, top-flight performance was localized in the semiconductor, consumer electronics, and automotive industries. A generation earlier, it was in shipbuilding, textiles, and steel. Today, it is in office equipment and electronic games.

Over time and at any given moment in time, a country does not prosper uniformly. Industries vary, and regions vary. In the United States, for example, with its rich mix of peoples and cultures, its loose federalism on the economic front, and its unusually good ability to adapt to changes in the key drivers of competitive success, regions are relatively free to work out their own road to prosperity—or to fall behind. There was once a booming textile industry in New England. Light manufacturing once flourished in New York City. Both are now gone. The heady mix of defense, energy, and entertainment industries that fueled the rapid post-war development of Los Angeles is a bit more problematic than it was a decade ago. Silicon Valley, which led the country and the world into the computer age, has new rivals in Texas and the mountain states. Once dominant urban centers—such as the Detroit of the glory days of the U.S. automobile industry—are now plagued with the seemingly intractable inner-city problems of drugs, violent crime, and decaying infrastructure.[16]

Similarly, even during the height of Japan's economic success, the vast majority of workers—in fact, 87 percent or more—were engaged in not very competitive industries.[17] To outside observers, only the world-class tip of the iceberg was visible. For most workers, the daily reality was altogether different. Nor was there much pressure to change. Because the few truly successful industries were such incredible engines of profit, the government had the resources to keep subsidizing weaker industries and weaker regions. It had the luxury—the mistaken luxury, it now seems—to prop them up rather than expose them to the rigors of global competition. Sheltered, they never grew tough—just ever more addicted to centrally provided support.

We are now paying the price for this false kindness. Our once mighty automotive and consumer electronics industries now look distinctly vulnerable. To revitalize themselves, they have had to transfer most of their operations outside the high-cost environment of Japan. In a fairly short period of time, the production capacity for three million cars a year has migrated to North America, and the production capacity for much of our consumer electronics to Southeast Asia. Much of what's left behind is the same old set of troubled, uncompetitive industries that cannot survive without subsidies—and that, when their markets are finally deregulated and opened, will die even with subsidies.

The much vaunted "Japan, Inc.," has so taken its success for granted that it does not really want to face—nor does it genuinely know how to face—the erosion of its ability to keep the charade of subsidy and protection going. High unemployment, declining tax income, extensive corporate restructuring—this is not the kind of environment to which the Japanese system can easily adapt. Even if it wanted to take corrective action, an individual company, for example, cannot sell off many of its real assets (because the government fears that doing so might depress land prices), cannot get rid of its equity holdings (because the Ministry of Finance fears that doing so might depress the

Nikkei index), and cannot lay off many of its workers (because the Ministry of Labor fears that doing so might trigger social unrest).

This is managerial gridlock on a large scale. More troubling, perhaps, it is not some new and unhappy development. Nor is it a set of unrelated problems that appeared suddenly and out of the blue. It is—and has been—part and parcel of Japan's "success" at every step along the way. The country as a whole was never competitive, remember. Just a handful of industries were. What kept the sluggish performance of the rest from marring the picture was not managerial competence or policy genius, but luck—and, of course, a decade and more of outrageously high land prices.

The story is, by now, familar. Because the supply of land in Japan is so limited, the prices associated with it rose during the 1980s by a factor of five. This unmanaged explosion of land values showed up on many companies' balance sheets as a huge increase in assets, which immediately translated into higher price/earnings ratios and those ratios, in turn, into much cheaper—even virtually "free"—sources of capital. Being human, Japanese managers and bankers took credit for these developments and treated them as resulting from sound judgment and careful action, not pure accident. With their competence so powerfully justified, they then took these resources and invested them with a massive lack of wisdom. Buoyed by so great a pool of liquidity, they built immense amounts of unnecessary capacity. What they did not do, however, was update their management structures and systems, globalize their organizations, or develop their people. With the golden goose so active in the laying house, why do anything other than feast continuously on omelette after omelette?

Today, of course, the illusion that made all this indulgence possible lies shattered. The debris is everywhere. Investments have turned sour, people are inadequately skilled, management systems remain ossified, and bank loans are delinquent; securities firms have burnt their fingers on the U.S. stock exchange, trading companies have burnt theirs in foreign exchange dealings, consumer electronics firms have burnt theirs in arrangements with Hollywood studios, and property developers have burnt theirs in real estate in Los Angeles, Hawaii, Pebble Beach, and New York. Where is MITI in all this? Or the Ministry of Finance? Or managerial panaceas like total quality management? Or

the armies of scholars who argued that Japan had solved the problems
of late-20th-century competition?

The answer is obvious: the sound and fury was just that—sound
and fury. None of it made all that much sense before, and none of it
does now. There are, indeed, successful, world-class Japanese companies from which managers around the globe do have much to learn.
But the same is true of Europe and the United States. Wherever you
look and whenever you look, only a few industries and a few companies prosper. That's it. Competitiveness is not—and simply cannot
be—the property of a nation state. In the borderless world, the key
factors for success depend increasingly on universal, not local, conditions.

At the margin, intelligent central government policy can certainly
help. Bad policy can hurt. But no policy can substitute for the efforts
of individual managers in individual institutions to link their activities
with the global economy. And no central government can sufficiently
free itself from the burden of both protection and the civil minimum
to embrace, let alone facilitate, those linkages. Nation states cannot
help but provide the locus and the fuel for the engine of "national interest." And that engine cannot help but drive the machinery of industrial decline. As the evidence shows, it is not a means for
harnessing the power of the global economy. Instead, it is a polished,
tested, and streamlined apparatus for creating ever-greater addiction to
centrally-provided support.

In an earlier age, to be sure, national interest meant something different. It used to provide a clear and unmistakable dividing line between what was ours and what was someone else's. This plot of land
is ours, not theirs; this factory is ours, not theirs; this company is
ours, not theirs. But how does this kind of logic apply today to a
Honda plant in Ohio or a Nissan plant in Tennessee or an IBM plant
in Japan or a Motorola plant in Malaysia? Whose "interests" does each
of these serve? The answer is far from clear.[18]

Or take a more controversial example: in 1971, the United States,
which had administered the island of Okinawa since the end of the
war in 1945, returned it to Japan. The Okinawans themselves, proud
of their independent Ryuku civilization and still mindful of their
forcible incorporation into Japan in the 19th century, were not uni-

formly enthusiastic. But for the Japanese, the return of Okinawa was an essential, if belated, act. It acknowledged sovereignty where sovereignty was due. Since then, of course, Japan has had to pour something like US $30 billion into a not yet successful effort to help the island become economically self-supporting.

Meanwhile, the Japanese government has not even been able to keep its northern island of Hokkaido busy with industry. It's tried shipbuilding; it's tried coal; it's tried pulp and paper; it's tried aluminum smelting; it's tried steel. Nothing has worked. Like Okinawa, Hokkaido still lives on US $20 billion worth of annual subsidies from Tokyo. And now, of course, bowing to intense political sentiment, Japan's weakened political leaders have decided to keep a wary distance from any productive relationship with the Russian government until it resolves the "northern territories" question—that is, until it returns the four islands of the Kuriles so that we can again pick up the tab for supporting them.

The emotion here is clear enough. So is the political posturing. And so is the so-called national interest. But where is the people's interest? Why should we worry about getting more islands back before we have figured out how to make the ones we already have work without endless subsidies? Where is the economic sense? Where is the hardheaded, objective concern for how best to improve the quality of life of Japanese citizens and consumers?

Chapter Six

SCARING THE GLOBAL ECONOMY AWAY

These substantive questions about where economic interest lies in a borderless world raise, in turn, a question of process. Are that world's major political units—its nation states—actually capable of addressing such interests in a fair way? Burdened as they are with electorally potent demands to provide the civil minimum and defend the national interest—in other words, with demands for subsidy and protection—do they have the flexibility, and the will, to make the hard and necessary choices? Equally important, do they still have the mechanisms in place to act on those choices if they really are able to make them?

With the ending of the Fifty Years' War between Soviet-style communism and the industrial democracies, the discipline exerted by both sides in that conflict has rapidly begun to erode. One result, noted previously, has been a marked upsurge in local and tribal conflicts. Supported by personal computers, mobile phones, fax machines, and a cache of arms, old loyalties have found renewed expression.

But these loyalties flow, for the most part, from the same patriotic sentiment and desire for independence that animated Western nation builders a century and more ago. Whether, if successful, they will lead to freestanding geographic units able to go it alone in a global economy is another matter entirely. It is not, for example, immediately obvious what would draw that economy to a proposed free-trade zone around Trincomalee harbor in an independent Tamil state in northern Sri Lanka. The aspirations are clear, but the jury will be out for a while.

The jury is already filing back in, however, to offer its verdict on a closely related case. The same erosion of Fifty Years' War discipline has fundamentally altered the challenge facing nation states. No longer is the key issue whether they are able to hold up their end, militarily if necessary, in this or that alliance. Nor is it whether, by pointing guns the wrong way, they are able to maintain control of their people. Nor is it whether they are able, by sovereign act, to speed up or slow down the expansion of free trade. They can. It is, rather, whether they are able to meet the same kind of test that will ultimately decide the fate of the splinter groups and rump countries described above. Can they draw the global economy in, leverage it productively, and keep it involved? On this key issue, the answer appears to be, not very well.

The Chinese government, for example, used to control its people and its regions through military power, the appointment of key personnel, and money. Today the global capital markets, the investment strategies of global corporations, and the growing autonomy of regional economic activities provide a discipline that prevents it from exercising control of this sort. If there were another event like Tiananmen Square, foreign capital would leave China, new foreign companies would not enter, and those already present would slow down or stop their provision of needed skills and technology. As the government in Beijing is all too uncomfortably aware, this might not put an end to the economic development of China, but it would certainly put a very sudden and abrupt end to the country's ability to develop at anything more than a snail's pace.[1]

This would be an intolerable outcome. Other countries—India, Indonesia, Argentina, and Brazil, for example—are increasingly in competition for as large a slice as possible of the same pie: the favorable "mind share" of global capital markets and of the CEOs of global companies. Given worldwide flows of information, the rising expectations of China's people for a better life, the continuing drain on resources represented by noncompetitive state-owned enterprises, and the country's own aspirations for regional or even global leadership, the Chinese government simply cannot risk another Tiananmen-like use of its military.

Nor can it exercise old-fashioned control through the power of money. In the past, it could extract whatever money it liked from state-owned enterprises and use that money to pacify opposition or buy support. Since goods and services never had real prices attached and no one knew what real costs were, the government could juggle the books as it liked. The opening up of the economy, however, has meant facing up to the fact that it can no longer do this. State-owned enterprises, once exposed to domestic competition from the newly established subsidiaries or joint ventures of leading global firms, can no longer afford to price in a vacuum. They have to start keeping real books, and real books put strict limits on the government's range of discretionary action.

Efforts by the central government to compensate for this loss of maneuvering room by introducing Western-style tax regimes are problematic. A recent attempt to introduce a value-added tax, for example, ended in confusion. More to the point, an effort to tax domestic corporations would produce little revenue since few make any money—well more than half, in fact, positively lose money. And an effort to make up the shortfall by heavily taxing foreign companies would only induce them either to leave or to ratchet down their in-country operations.

In China, until very recently, there was no term for unemployment. What people spoke about instead was *taiye* or "waiting for assignment." Such euphemisms will no longer suffice. Beijing will have to face this—and other—economic issues squarely and honestly. When it does, however, it will become clear to everyone that Beijing does not have the answer. Nor should it. This is not a nation state-specific "problem" that the central government is somehow obligated to solve entirely on its own. It is a problem that affects the whole global economy.

Thus, Chinese leaders can reasonably look to that global network of economic activity for help in defining and addressing their problems. For their part, the leading players in that network will see it to be in their own self-interest to help. If China's economic modernization slows down or fails, everyone will suffer from the loss of attractive new markets. Similarly, if it succeeds but in a careless and irresponsible way, the resulting pollution of the environment and flood of imitation products will also affect everyone. Put simply, the "China problem" is not China's problem alone. In the borderless economy of an interdependent world, there need not be any such thing as local sovereignty over local difficulties. The global economy can help provide solutions. It will not need to be coaxed; it will want to do so. The question, rather, is whether government will seek out and accept such help—and whether it will so organize itself as to make both the seeking and the acceptance effective and efficient.

To do this, China will have to proceed much further down the road of granting regional autonomy in economic matters. Equally important, it will have to redefine the role of the central government. On both fronts, the country has made far better progress than Russia. Even so, its efforts to date have been piecemeal and ad hoc. The logic underlying them has not been fully worked out, nor has adherence to it been either universal or consistent. But it is only such a logic—an explicit commitment to heightened regional autonomy within a "commonwealth" of China—that will free up the energies needed to harness the support of the global economy. If Beijing could embrace the idea of becoming the *chunghwa,* or "prosperous center land," in a commonwealth of regional entities, confidence everywhere would go up, global support would pour in, and a precedent would be established for the long-term integration of Hong Kong and Taiwan.

Time is short. Inflationary pressures have again begun to overheat the development engine. Global firms are actively debating how rapidly to expand their operations and aspirations inside China. Huge income disparities—disparities measured by a factor of 20 or more—have opened between inland and coastal regions. Proposed founding membership in the World Trade Organization depends on much greater openness of markets. The future political direction of Taiwan is even now being redefined. Hong Kong reverts back to Chinese control in 1997. The questions, therefore, have to be answered.

First, just how serious is China about treating the global economy not as a useful if intrusive presence to be kept at arm's length, but as a—perhaps the only—real source of the talent, resources, and energy

needed to build a better life for its people? And second, just how willing are the leaders in Beijing to ignore the old reflexes of sovereignty
and central control in forging meaningful links with that economy?

China is, perhaps, an extreme example, but the verdict does have
general applicability: the old means of control no longer work and can
no longer be used with impunity. They will simply scare the global
economy away, and active participation by that economy is essential
to development in a borderless world. Unless they choose to wall
themselves off from it entirely, as North Korea has more or less done
(although funds still come in, unofficially of course, from arms sales
abroad and from large numbers of Koreans in Japan), governments
have simply lost the power to keep the global capital markets at bay
(see Appendix A). At the same time, they still retain—but are gradual-
ly losing—the power to keep their domestic markets closed both to
foreign goods and to direct participation by foreign companies.

That there will be pressure to keep all this at arm's length is predictable. Politically influential constituencies will always exist that
favor the civil minimum and protection in the name of the national interest. The test for governments of nation states is not whether such
pressures arise, but whether they have the will—and the ability—to
resist them and to embrace, not just grudgingly accept, the global
economy. Again, the verdict so far is, in most cases, probably not.

The liberal industrial democracies, in particular, have developed in
a way that seems to put both will and ability ever further out of reach.
Consider, first, the notion of traditional liberalism itself, that great
foundation stone of the modern nation state in the West. The essence
of the liberal ideal in civic life is philosophical support, backed up by
extensive public investments in education, for both responsible individual action and cultural diversity—except where either conflicts directly with the broader public good. In practical terms, this defines
the implicit charter between government and governed in terms of the
former's commitment, having supplied the necessary educational resources, to tolerate and respect a teeming pluralism of style and aspiration in exchange for the latter's commitment both to extend that
same courtesy to others and to defer, without divisive haggling, on
those limited occasions when the public good really does demand
both obedience and support.

Historically, the classic liberal ideal represents a genuine, creative effort to deal fairly and honorably with an unprecedented level of social pluralism—that is, to strike an altogether new, workable balance between the uniformity of behavior traditionally demanded of citizens by the state and the limited unity of purpose those states genuinely require to survive and prosper in the contemporary world.

For this ideal to work in practice, however, there must be mutual respect (so that differences in style or preference are not interpreted as a threatening challenge), mutual trust (so that actions are not interpreted as a narrow-minded imposition on others), and transparent information (so that all members of society can be confident of the essential fairness of what gets decided, even if they do not particularly like it). Judgments by the state inevitably limit some individual's or some group's freedom. All citizens, for example, may want to be able to drive a car to work in a crowded, urban business district. But, in the general public interest, there may have to be restrictions on their unfettered ability to do so. Experience shows that such restrictions are most readily accepted when they—and the process of debate leading up to them—meet the three criteria noted above.

In most cases, neither private behavior nor government action in the liberal democracies today meets these criteria. Given thoroughly inadequate investments in education, even the core value of pluralism has become suspect because it might give an advantage to someone else's group. Civic responsibility has largely disappeared. In its place, as discussed previously, has evolved self-interested competition among issue-focused interest groups, which lack both mutual respect and mutual trust. In recent local elections in Japan, only about 30 percent of the eligible population voted. That means, in practice, that an organized group of 16 people out of every hundred eligible voters can effectively play the role of a democratic majority, dominate the public agenda, and ensure preferential treatment of its own interests. Because these voters have the numbers, they do not have to listen to others, and they do not have to respond.

Worse still, given the nuts-and-bolts mechanics of how decisions actually get made, information has become opaque, not transparent. On the vast majority of topics, an "iron triangle" of lawmakers, bureaucrats, and special interests dominates the process.[2] Thus, decisions about urban traffic restrictions disproportionately tend to reflect the influential voices of garage and parking lot owners, say, or of developers whose property would increase in value if new commuter rail lines were to be built. Drivers licenses, *which cost well over $2,000 in Japan,* cannot be freed up because of powerful lobbying by the driving schools. Expensive car inspections cannot be removed because of the need to keep automobile repair shops fully fed. As a result, few members of these societies are comfortable with the judgments among competing interests that ultimately get made.

Lacking comfort, members of democratic societies lack comity. Lacking comity, they have no motivation to strive for—or accept—a reasonable balance among competing demands. For the individual, the only relevant standard quickly becomes no more and no less than "whether, right now, today, I get mine." And when such a standard is in force, the pluralist ethos of liberalism irreparably decays. Long-term decisions in the communal interest—decisions, for example, in favor of putting global logic first—can rarely get made.

This collapse of liberalism is, obviously, a large part of the reason why the industrial democracies find it so hard to open themselves actively to the borderless economy. Now, the implications of this collapse could be offset, to some degree, if political leaders came to office deeply schooled and experienced in the complex dynamics of that economy, or if they were better able to withstand such pressures and so provide a constituency for global logic. But they do not and cannot.

In a political arena increasingly dominated by television and other media, it matters profoundly that the average Japanese and American viewer's span of TV attention is 15 and 12 seconds, respectively. Politics by sound bite simply do not permit sophisticated "common good" arguments in favor of global logic. They do, however, both permit and encourage a high level of attention to be paid to the self-interested demands of vocal, powerful groups. With few exceptions, centrifugal forces are in the saddle, and they scare the global economy away. It does not have to be this way (see Appendix B).

On balance, then, precisely at a time when the economic well-being of people around the world increasingly depends on their ability to participate in the global economy, the nation states in which they live find it both structurally and philosophically difficult to offer systemic, continuous support for such participation. The record, of course, is not entirely dark. The recent agreements on NAFTA and GATT, as well as the verbal commitment of APEC to trade liberalization, are all to the good. Modern nation states, however, will find it hard to escape for long either the backward pull of national interest and the civil minimum or the fragmentation of communal interest represented by the collapse of traditional liberalism.

This is, in an important sense, not a new problem. Writing about much the same issue of competing, factional interests under the pseudonym Publius more than two centuries ago, James Madison noted in the Tenth Federalist Paper that "it is in vain to say that enlightened statesmen will be able to adjust these clashing interests, and render them all subservient to the public good. Enlightened statesmen will not always be at the helm." As a result, he argued, the only intelligent and responsible course—the course represented, in his day, by ratification of a federal constitution—was to accept the fact that "the *causes* of faction cannot be removed, and that relief is only to be sought in the means of controlling its *effects*." For Madison, this meant building a republic large enough that no single interest could dominate and that varied and competing interests would balance each other out.

The danger against which Madison sought to create a practical defense was the historical tendency of majorities under such forms of government to impose their will on the minority. In this, he succeeded. He did not inquire, however, what was best to do when this balancing among factions led not to a refined, synthesized vision of the long-term common good, but to a continual focus on interests so separate, short-term, and disconnected that no coherent vision of the common good could be agreed upon, much less implemented. In today's borderless economy, however, that is precisely the question facing nation states. And, on the evidence to date, it is a question they are markedly failing to answer.

Chapter Seven

THE EMERGENCE OF REGION STATES

As the previous chapters have shown, the glue holding traditional nation states together, at least in economic terms, has begun to dissolve. Buffeted by sudden changes in industry dynamics, available information, consumer preferences, and flows of capital; burdened by demands for the civil minimum and for open-ended subsidies in the name of the national interest; and hog-tied by political systems that prove ever-less responsive to new challenges, these political aggregations no longer make compelling sense as discrete, meaningful units on an up-to-date map of economic activity. They are still there, of course, still major players on the world stage. But they have, for the most part, lost the ability to put global logic first in the decisions they make.

For nation states and especially for their leaders, the primary issue remains protection—of territory, of resources, of jobs, of industries, even of ideology. In Guangzhou, however, the capital of the state of Guangdong, young Chinese ladies have something else on their minds: Avon lipstick. Some time back, Avon ran a TV commercial that implied that Cantonese girls, if they managed to get a hold of Avon products, could easily be as attractive as Hong Kong girls. With the right makeup and, perhaps, the right (suitably short) outfit, a happy world of clubs and music and dancing and romance was theirs for the taking.

The result: there are now more than 30,000 Avon ladies selling products door-to-door in Guangdong alone; in Shanghai, where operations have just started, there are another 6,000. These salespeople, no less than the girls eagerly snatching up their wares, probably do not remember how to spell "communism" any more. Their minds are on the possibilities suddenly open to them through the global market, not on the backward-looking concerns of the nation state to which they belong.

By contrast, the territorial dividing lines that do make sense belong to what I call "region states"—geographical units like northern Italy; Baden-Würtemberg (or the upper Rhine);[1] Wales; San Diego/Tijuana; Hong Kong/southern China; the Silicon Valley/Bay Area in California; and Pusan (at the southern tip of the Korean peninsula) and the cities of Fukuoka and Kitakyushu in the north of the Japanese island of Kyushu. Other such areas include the Growth Triangle of Singapore, Johore (the southernmost state of Malaysia), and the neighboring Riau Islands of Indonesia (including Batam, a large tax-free zone); Research Triangle Park in North Carolina; the Rhône-Alps region of France, centered on Lyons, with its tight business and cultural ties to Italy; the Languedoc-Roussillon region, centered on Toulouse, with its tight linkages with Catalonia; Tokyo and its outlying areas; Osaka and the Kansai region; the Malaysian island of Penang (see Appendix C); and even the newly emerging Greater Growth Triangle, unveiled in 1992 across the Strait of Malacca, connecting Penang, Medan (an Indonesian city in Sumatra), and Phuket in Thailand.

In a borderless world, these are the natural economic zones. Though limited in geographical size, they are often huge in their economic influence. As Exhibit 8–2 indicates, for example, Japan's Shutoken region—Tokyo and the three immediately neighboring prefectures—has a cumulative GNP that, were it a full-blown nation state, would rank it third worldwide after the United States and Germany. Similarly, Japan's Kansai region—Osaka, Kobe, and Kyoto—would rank sixth, just after the U.K. Instead of being able to join the G-7, however, Kansai's mayors and governors must commute weekly to Tokyo, hat in hand, to get approval and permission and resources for whatever they want to do. Not only do regional leaders in Japan not get to take the seat at the global table to which their economies ought to entitle them, they do not even enjoy the same regional freedoms that leaders of the states in the United States and of the *Länder* in Germany do.

These region states may or may not fall within the borders of a particular nation. Whether they do is purely an accident of history. In practical terms, it really does not matter. Like Singapore, many are, in effect, city states, which have willingly—and explicitly—given up some of the trappings of nation states in return for the (relatively) unfettered ability to tap extensively into the four I's of the global economy.

Region states are not, however, the same thing—although they may be the same size—as a megacity like Calcutta or Mexico City. Unlike region states, these immense human aggregations either do not or cannot look to the global economy for solutions to their problems or for the resources to make those solutions work. They look, instead, to the central governments of the nation states in which they reside.

By virtue of their political subordination, megacities are immune to global logic, neither seeking it out nor able to harness it when available. Absent these global linkages, however, they are, as a rule, unable to bootstrap themselves back onto a healthy trajectory of growth. In effect, deference to sovereignty isolates them and robs them of the only workable means for improvement. At the same time, deference to sovereignty imposes a huge, often unsupportable burden on their central governments, which—consistent with the civil minimum—must pour endless resources into their bottomless pits of need. Thus, as with declining industries, the economic dynamics of megacities graph a downward spiral from which there is no self-contained escape. Region states are different in that they gladly sidestep the bunting and hoopla of sovereignty in return for the ability to harness the global I's to their own needs.

Population, then, is not the key issue. What matters most is that each region state possesses, in one or another combination, the essential ingredients for successful participation in the global economy. With only 2.5 million people (70 percent Chinese, 20 percent Malay, and 10 percent Indian) and virtually no natural resources, Singapore—by natural endowment, a kind of Costa Rica in Asia—simply could not have prospered without inviting in the global economy. Its sister island of Penang has learned the lesson well. (See Appendix C, reprinted from a recent issue of the *Wall Street Journal,* about the development of

Penang, Malaysia. It is broadly typical of a growing number of stories about regional development efforts.) Both have had the wisdom and the will—and the determination—to put global logic first.

A FLOWERING OF REGIONS

Just look, for example, at what is happening in Southeast Asia as the Hong Kong economy reaches out to embrace first Shenzhen and then other parts of the Pearl River Delta. Hong Kong, where GNP per capita is roughly US $12,000, is now the driving economic force in the lives of the people in Shenzhen, whose GNP per capita has already been boosted to US $5,695 by the radiating effects of these linkages. (For China as a whole, the comparable figure is US $317.) Even today, these linkages are not limited to Shenzhen, but reach out to include Zhuhai, Amoy, and Guangzhou as well (see Exhibit 7–1). By the year

EXHIBIT 7–1

The Structure of a Region State

(Per capita GNP; US $

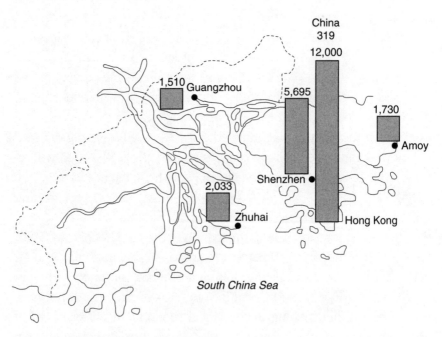

Source: China Annual Statistics; Bank of Japan.

EXHIBIT 7–2

The Dynamism of Hong Kong and Neighboring Areas

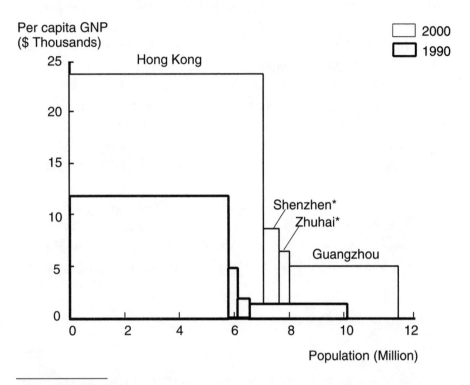

*Special economic zone only.

Note: The projected amounts assume that each area will continue growing at 1980–89 rates.

Source: China Statistic Annual; Asian Development Bank; *Economist; Ethnic Chinese Overseas*, Chung-Hsun Yu; McKinsey analysis.

2000, as Exhibit 7–2 indicates, this cross-border region state will have raised the standard of living of more than 11 million people over the US $5000 level.

Chinese officials seem to have gotten the message, at least in part. They have already expanded the special economic zone concept, which has worked so well for Shenzhen and Shanghai, to 14 other areas, many of them inland. One such project, at Yunnan, will become a cross-border economic zone encompassing Laos and Vietnam. In Vietnam itself, Ho Chi Minh City has launched a similar effort, Sepzone, to attract foreign capital.

As Exhibit 7–3 indicates, still other initiatives are in the works. In northern Asia, for example, the currently stalled Tumen Delta project, if it materializes, will cut across China, North Korea, and Russia. In Japan, there is much interest in a Sea of Japan Economic Zone or a Northeastern Asia Economic Zone, which would connect the Russian cities of Nakhodka, Khabarovsk, and Vladivostok with the Japanese city of Niigata. There is also an idea to create an Integrated Northeast Asia Economic Zone that, were it to come to fruition, would link the Tumen Delta project with the Northeastern Asia project.

Though still in the concept stage, these undertakings have already begun to change the old Cold War mentality separating Russian and Japanese officials. There is already a regular ferry service across the Sea of Japan, as well as active discussion about establishing a ferry between Wakkanai on Hokkaido and Yuzhno-Sakhalinsk on Sakhalin. If this were to happen, the city of Vanino, across the Strait of Mamiya from Sakhalin, would become the best port for loading Japanese

EXHIBIT 7–3

Emerging Regional Couplings

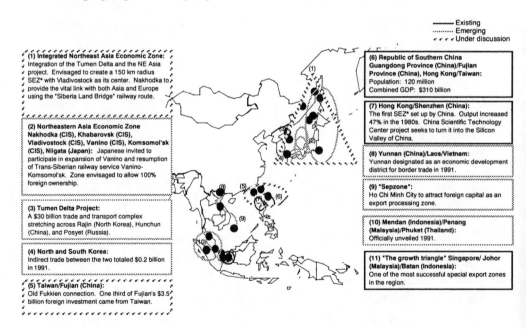

——— Existing
·········· Emerging
ϵ ϵ ϵ Under discussion

(1) Integrated Northeast Asia Economic Zone: Integration of the Tumen Delta and the NE Asia project. Envisaged to create a 150 km radius SEZ* with Vladivostock as its center. Nakhodka to provide the vital link with both Asia and Europe using the "Siberia Land Bridge" railway route.

(2) Northeastern Asia Economic Zone Nakhodka (CIS), Khabarovsk (CIS), Vladivostock (CIS), Vanino (CIS), Komsomol'sk (CIS), Niigata (Japan): Japanese invited to participate in expansion of Vanino and resumption of Trans-Siberian railway service Vanino-Komsomol'sk. Zone envisaged to allow 100% foreign ownership.

(3) Tumen Delta Project: A $30 billion trade and transport complex stretching across Rajin (North Korea), Hunchun (China), and Posyet (Russia).

(4) North and South Korea: Indirect trade between the two totaled $0.2 billion in 1991.

(5) Taiwan/Fujian (China): Old Fukkien connection. One third of Fujian's $3.5 billion foreign investment came from Taiwan.

(6) Republic of Southern China Guangdong Province (China)/Fujian Province (China), Hong Kong/Taiwan: Population: 120 million Combined GDP: $310 billion

(7) Hong Kong/Shenzhen (China): The first SEZ* set up by China. Output increased 47% in the 1980s. China Scientific Technology Center project seeks to turn it into the Silicon Valley of China.

(8) Yunnan (China)/Laos/Vietnam: Yunnan designated as an economic development district for border trade in 1991.

(9) "Sepzone": Ho Chi Minh City to attract foreign capital as an export processing zone.

(10) Mendan (Indonesia)/Penang (Malaysia)/Phuket (Thailand): Officially unveiled 1991.

(11) "The growth triangle" Singapore/ Johor (Malaysia)/Batan (Indonesia): One of the most successful special export zones in the region.

*SEZ=Special Economic Zone.

goods bound for Europe on the Siberian Railway and for off-loading European goods bound for Japan.

On China's Liaodong Peninsula, the city of Dalian, together with its hinterland around Shenyang, is host to more than 3,500 active corporations—nearly 2,500 of which are foreign-affiliated, including 250 or so that are Japanese. Because the Chinese government still has not officially forgiven Japan for its wartime actions, Japanese songs, books, and movies are, if not exactly prohibited, strongly discouraged. In Dalian, however, the second most popular foreign language chosen by high school students is Japanese, and the artifacts of its culture are readily available.

This is because Bo Xilai, the mayor of Dalian, knows perfectly well that continued economic growth depends on providing an attractive home for foreign investment. He also knows that the region's leaders cannot responsibly ignore the needs of these foreign operations in favor of protecting the many state-owned enterprises that are losing money. Dalian, its people, and its hopes for a brighter economic future simply cannot afford it.

As Exhibit 7–4 illustrates, Dalian is rapidly becoming a part of the global economy in its own right. Capital and corporations from literally all over the world are flowing to its new industrial development area, which is adjacent to the old city. By the year 2000, this new development will hold more than two million people, bringing Dalian's total to over 7.2 million. With the highway linking it to the inland city of Shenyang now complete, the emergent region state of Liaoning Province, including Dalian, has access to an extremely talented and hardworking northern Chinese labor force. If the central powers in Beijing do not intervene, this will give it a sound basis for participating in—and pulling in resources from—the global economy. Given this situation, it is only natural that people in Dalian now feel that prosperity is created from without, not from the national center. Much the same is true in other parts of China—Tianjin, Qingdao, and Wuhan, for example. Indeed, some of the northeastern provinces have already reached a steeper learning curve than Japan—with higher productivity and only 2–3 *percent* of comparable wage levels—in the manufacture both of printed circuit boards for laptop computers and of cylinder heads for videocassette recorders.

EXHIBIT 7–4

Foreign Investment in Dalian Industrial Development Zone
(Cumulative in $ millions; October 1984–December 1993)

No.	Country	Number	Total Investment	Total paid-in capital	Pain-in capital by foreigners
1	Japan	207	1,388.9	705.7	538.5
2	Hong Kong	388	2,113.4	1,062.5	455.8
3	U.S.A.	127	695.4	426.1	202.3
4	Taiwan	76	179.1	128.4	58.8
5	South Korea	39	71.0	48.9	28.7
6	Singapore	21	80.2	62.5	17.8
7	Macao	16	93.7	65.3	15.6
8	Thailand	15	42.4	28.8	11.4
9	Malaysia	12	31.9	21.1	11.9
10	Canada	9	56.2	42.8	6.5
11	Russia	7	45.7	42.8	7.7
12	Italy	7	15.7	13.7	7.2
13	France	4	751.4	204.6	41.3
14	Bolivia	7	55.0	26.1	9.2
15	Australia	3	3.2	2.3	1.2
16	U.K.	3	3.3	2.6	0.6
17	Argentina	2	13.1	5.5	1.4
18	New Zealand	2	5.5	3.0	1.5
19	North Korea	2	3.0	2.1	1.3

It is from regionally bounded areas such as these that the lion's share of future economic growth will come. Nation states will not drive it. They cannot. In a borderless economy, as we have seen, too much accumulated baggage weighs them down. Even in Asia, where the postwar "miracle" of Japan's—and, more recently, the Four Tigers'—explosive development provides a much studied model of success, other countries will find it increasingly difficult to follow the same course. There is no longer any single head bird in the flock of Asian "flying geese." The situation is different now. There are various possible models to follow. Thailand, not Japan, may chart the course for Myanmar and Vietnam.

One reason for this is that economic competition is now far more immediate as well as far more global. Another is that the contest for a finite pool of inward investment is more intense, and the advantage conferred by low-cost labor is more fleeting. At each stage of its growth, for example, Japan had to compete with only a limited num-

EXHIBIT 7–5

Number of Countries in the Development Queue
(Percent)

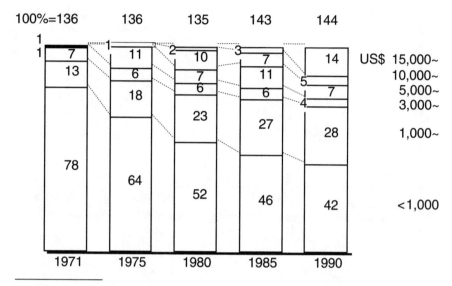

Note: This figure refers to nations whose GNP data are available among the World Bank members.

Source: *World Tables 1993*, World Bank.

ber of countries in the "development queue." Today, however, the emerging economies—especially those in the critical, "takeoff" range of US $1,000 to $3,000 per capita—are far from alone (see Exhibit 7–5). In addition, Japan was able to leverage the benefits of its low-cost labor for several decades. More recently, South Korea and Singapore, by contrast, enjoyed comparable benefits for a much shorter period of time. At present, the coastal regions of China, which have really just gotten on the development map, are already beginning to price themselves out of the running, compared with inland areas and with countries like Vietnam and, before too long, Myanmar.

Moreover, as Exhibit 7–6 illustrates (see also Exhibit 7–7), the absolute gap in GNP per capita between developed and developing economies has substantially widened. In other words, the road has gotten tougher *at the same time that* the hurdle has gotten higher. *And*

EXHIBIT 7–6

Stages of Economic Development

(US $ thousands)

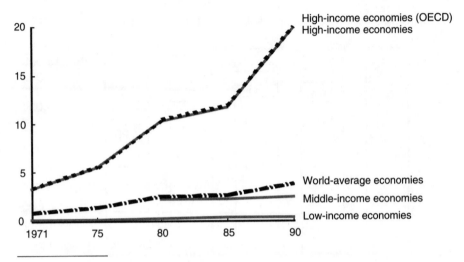

Source: World Tables 1993, World Bank.

at the same time that political resistance to low-cost imports is rising in traditional importing countries. Encumbered as they are, the region's nation states will not be able to close this gap. Nor will they be able to generate the additional US $2 trillion or so per year—the equivalent of about 20 additional Hong Kongs—needed to bring the overall Asian economy to a par with that of NAFTA or the EU.

If, however, these nation states do not try to do everything themselves but allow, literally, the creation of 20 additional Hong Kongs—that is, if they support and encourage the development of region states within and across their borders—the US $2 trillion goal is well within reach. And that, in turn, means lifting a total of some 213 million people over the US $5,000 GNP per capita level by the end of the decade—a number that compares quite favorably with the likely end-of-the-decade situation in NAFTA (278 million) and the EU (361 million).

PORTS OF ENTRY

"All politics," as Tip O'Neill, former Speaker of the U.S. House of Representatives, was wont to say, "is local." Region states, however, are economic not political units, and they are anything but local in focus. They may lie within the borders of an established nation state, but they are such powerful engines of development because their primary orientation is toward—and their primary linkage is with—the global economy. They are, in fact, among its most reliable ports of entry.

Region states welcome foreign investment. They welcome foreign ownership. They welcome foreign products. In fact, they welcome whatever will help employ their people productively, improve their quality of life, and give them access to the best and cheapest products from anywhere in the world. And they have learned that such access is often best and easiest when the products are not produced at home. (Singaporeans, for example, enjoy better and cheaper agricultural products than do the Japanese, although Singapore has no farmers—and no farms—of its own.) Region states also welcome the chance to use whatever surplus these activities generate to ratchet up their people's quality of life still further, not to fund the civil minimum or subsidize outmoded industries. Their leaders do not show up somewhere in the world trying to attract factories and investment and then appear on TV back home vowing to protect local companies no matter what. In a word, they consistently put global logic first.

Region states make such effective ports of entry to the global economy because the very characteristics that define them are shaped by the demands of that economy. They must, for example, be large enough to provide an attractive market for the brand development of leading consumer products. Hence, they tend to be between 5 and 20 million people in size. The range is broad, but the extremes are clear: not half a million, not 50 or 100 million. That is because they must be small enough for their citizens to share interests as consumers, but still of sufficient size to justify economies not of scale (which, after all, can be leveraged from a base of any size through exports to the rest of the world), but of service—that is, the infrastructure of communications, transportation, and professional services essential to participation in the global economy. (They must have, for example, at least one international airport and, more than likely, one good harbor with international-class freight-handling facilities.)

As the reach of TV expands, advertising becomes efficient. Although trying to achieve penetration of a consumer brand throughout all of Japan or Indonesia may be prohibitively expensive, establishing it firmly in the Osaka[2] or Jakarta regions is far more affordable—and

EXHIBIT 7-7

Classification of Economies by Income and Region, 1992–1993

Income group	Subgroup	Sub-Saharan Africa[1]		Asia		Europe and Central Asia		Middle East and North Africa		Americas
		East and Southern Africa	West Africa	East Asia and Pacific	South Asia	Eastern Europe and Central Asia	Rest of Europe	Middle East	North Africa	
Low-income		Burundi	Benin	Cambodia	Afghanistan			Yemen	Egypt	Guyana
		Comoros	Burkina Faso	China	Bangladesh					Haiti
		Ethiopia	Central	Indonesia	Bhutan					Honduras
		Kenya	African Rep	Laos	India					Nicaragua
		Lesotho	Chad	Myanmar	Maldives					
		Madagascar	Equatorial	Solomon	Nepal					
		Malawi	Guinea	Islands	Pakistan					
		Mozambique	Gambia	Vietnam	Sri Lanka					
		Rwanda	Ghana							
		Somalia	Guinea							
		Sudan	Guinea-							
		Tanzania	Bissau							
		Uganda	Liberia							
		Zaire	Mali							
		Zambia	Mauritania							
		Zimbabwe	Niger							
			Nigeria							
			São Tomé							
			and Principe							
			Sierra Leone							
			Togo							

Middle-income	Lower	Angola Djibouti Mauritius Namibia Swaziland	Cameroon Cape Verde Congo Ivory Coast Senegal	Fiji Kiribati Korea, Dem. Rep. Malaysia Marshall Islands Micronesia Mongolia Papua New Guinea Philippines Thailand Tonga Vanuatu Western Samoa	Albania Armenia Azerbaijan Bulgaria Czecho-slovakia[2] Georgia Kazakhstan Kyrgyzstan Moldova Poland Romania Tajikistan Turkmenistan Ukraine Uzbekistan	Turkey	Iran Iraq Jordan Lebanon Syria	Algeria Morocco Tunisia	Belize Bolivia Chile Colombia Costa Rica Cuba Dominica Dominican Rep. Ecuador El Salvador Grenada Guatemala Jamaica Panama Paraguay Peru St. Lucia St. Vincent
	Upper	Botswana Mayotte Reunion Seychelles South Africa	Gabon	American Samoa Guam Korea, Rep. Macao New Caledonia	Belarus Estonia Hungary Latvia Lithuania Russian Federation Yugoslavia[3]	Gibraltar Greece Isle of Man Malta Portugal	Bahrain Oman Saudi Arabia	Libya	Antigua and Barbuda Argentina Aruba Barbados Brazil French Guiana Guadeloupe Martinique Mexico Netherlands Antilles Puerto Rico St. Kitts and Nevis Suriname Trinidad and Tobago Uruguay Venezuela
No. of low- and middle-income economies: 162		26	23	25	8	6	9	5	38

EXHIBIT 7-7 (Continued)

Income group	Subgroup	East and Southern Africa	West Africa	East Asia and Pacific	South Asia	Eastern Europe and Central Asia	Rest of Europe	Middle East	North Africa	Americas
		Sub-Saharan Africa[1]		Asia		Europe and Central Asia		Middle East and North Africa		Americas
High-income	OECD countries			Australia Japan New Zealand			Andorra Austria Belgium Denmark Finland France Germany Iceland Ireland Italy Luxembourg Netherlands Norway San Marino Spain Sweden Switzerland UK			Canada United States
	Non-OECD countries			Brunei French Polynesia Hong Kong Singapore OAE[4]			Channel Islands Cyprus Faeroe Islands Greenland	Israel Kuwait Qatar United Arab Emirates		Bahamas Bermuda Virgin Islands (U.S.)
Total no. of economies: 201		26	23	33	8	22	28	13	5	43

Definitions of groups

These tables classify all World Bank member economies, plus all other economies with populations of more than 30,000.

Income group: Economies are divided according to 1991 GNP per capita, calculated using the World Bank Atlas method. The groups are: low-income, $635 or less; lower-middle-income, $636–$2,555; upper-middle-income, $2,556–$7,910; and high-income, $7,911 or more. The estimates for the republics of the former Soviet Union should be regarded as very preliminary; their classification will be kept under review.

[1]For some analyses, South Africa is not included in Sub-Saharan Africa.
[2]Refers to the former Czechoslovakia; disaggregated data are not yet available.
[3]Refers to the former Socialist Federal Republic of Yugoslavia; disaggregated data are not yet available.
[4]Other Asian economies, e.g., Taiwan, China.

far more likely to generate handsome returns. Much the same is true with sales and service networks, customer satisfaction programs, market surveys, and management information systems: efficient scale is to be found at the regional, not the national, level. This matters because, on balance, it is modern marketing techniques that shape the economies of region states. For individual companies, political borders are little more than an artificial, externally imposed source of inefficiency. What counts, instead, is the geographical clustering of broad similarities in taste and preference.

In order to sell branded consumer goods, for example, TV advertising is essential. Something like 100,000 gross rating points (GRP) are needed to establish a reasonable level of brand recognition. But the cost of such advertising is sufficiently high that it can be justified only when it reaches a large enough audience—say, several million potential consumers. After the brand is established, the next step is to get all the other essential pieces in place: shelf control in retail outlets, just-in-time delivery, after-sales service, cooperative promotions with local retailers, and the like. This means setting up a logistics and marketing operation dedicated to the region—again an expensive undertaking justified only by the potential size of the market. Thus, if the market is too small, it cannot get over the threshold to qualify as a stand-alone region state. Conversely, if it is so large—either in population or geographical extent—that several parallel operations systems are required to service it, it lacks the focused coherence to qualify as a region state.

Where true economies of service exist, religious, ethnic, and racial distinctions are not important—or at least, they are of as little importance as human nature allows. Singapore is 70 percent ethnic Chinese, but its 30 percent minority is no problem because commercial prosperity creates sufficient affluence to keep them contented. Nor are ethnic differences a source of concern for potential investors. In Indonesia, however, with its 250 or so different tribal groups, 18,000 islands, and 188 million people, no organization theory known to man can define a mode of political order secure or stable enough to calm all investors' fears.

Still, Indonesia has traditionally attempted to impose a single form of political order from the center by applying fictional averages. They do not work.[3] But if the country's leaders allowed economies of service to define, within Indonesia, two or three Singapore-sized region states, they *could* be managed. A recent (1991) effort to make Batam Island an open economy linked with Singapore has already attracted more than 50 foreign corporations, mostly from Japan. A comparable effort in Medan is now under way. If successful, these initiatives spearheaded by President Suharto, would work against, rather than exacerbate, the country's manifold social divisions.

Indeed, because the orientation of region states is toward the global economy, not toward their host nations, they help breed an internationalism of outlook that defuses many of the usual kinds of social tensions. In the United States, for example, the Japanese have already established about 120 "transplant" auto industry-related factories throughout the Mississippi Valley. More are on the way. As their share of the domestic industry's production grows, people in the region, who look to these plants for their livelihoods and for the tax revenues to support their local communities, will stop caring whether the plants belong to U.S.- or Japan-headquartered companies. All they will care about are the economic benefits of having them there—in the Valley Region State.

The mere existence of relevant service economies does not, of course, mean that a region will always act—or even aspire to act—as a local outpost of the global economy. As already noted briefly in Chapter 5, Annalee Saxenian has shown that,[4] for much of its history, Silicon Valley in California, that great engine of much of the microelectronics industry in the United States, prospered—especially by comparison with that other regional center of microelectronics, Route 128 in Massachusetts—because its laid-back, freewheeling style attracted top-flight people, ideas, and venture capitalists and allowed them to combine and recombine in a "networked" industrial model. By providing an open, local point of connection to the fast-moving, worldwide universe of technology and technologists, it quickly outpaced its Massachusetts rival (see Exhibit 7–8).

By contrast, Route 128 went to Washington as it were, turned lobbyist, studied "competitiveness" as a way to get more federal funding for R&D, and grew protectionist. It has also begun to discourage, even bar, foreign investments as well as foreign takeovers. The inevitable result: Japan is now developing a Silicon Island on Kyushu; Taiwan is

EXHIBIT 7–8

Employment in Electronic Components and Semiconductor Firms
(*Silicon Valley and Route 128, 1959–1980*)

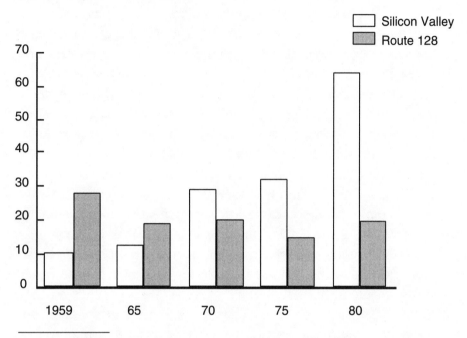

Source: County Business Patterns.

trying to create a Silicon Island of its own; and Korea is nurturing a Silicon Peninsula. This is the worst of all possible outcomes: less new money in Massachusetts and a host of newly energized and well-funded competitive areas.

Such defensiveness is the detritus of old suspicions. It very much gets in the way. But it does not have to. When, for example, Hollywood recognized that it was about to face a severe capital shortage, it did not throw up protectionist barriers against foreign money. Instead, it invited Rupert Murdoch into 20th-Century-Fox, C. Itoh and Toshiba into Time-Warner, Sony into Columbia, and Matsushita into MCA. The result: a $15 billion infusion of new capital—and, equally important, $15 billion less for Japan or anyone else to set up a competing Hollywood of its own.

These experiences do not argue for entrusting all efforts to forge productive linkages with the global economy to the fragmented, idiosyncratic choices of individual companies. They certainly do not argue for getting government, at any level, involved in picking those industries or technologies that should be so linked. Between the extremes of centrally directed industrial policy and hands-off free markets, however, there is room for regional policy. Done well, this can easily make the difference between local prosperity and local versions of nation state-type paralysis. The trick, as Saxenian notes, is to develop policies that "help companies to learn and respond quickly to changing conditions—rather than policies that either protect or isolate them from competition or external change." The goal, in other words, is to foster the development of flexible communities of interest through local networks. These networks provide multiple forums for collaboration and the exchange of opinions. But, in aggregate, they also make possible the economies of service that legitimize region-based infrastructure for communicating with—and connecting to—the global economy.

The heart of the challenge, remember, is not to solve all problems locally, but rather to make it possible to solve them by harnessing global resources. The effectiveness of region states depends on their ability to tap global solutions. When nation states were the dominant actors in economic affairs, a potential infusion of new resources or new talent was not always welcome: there might be vested interests to protect or suspicions of foreign influence to gratify for political ends. Region states, by contrast, carry virtually none of this baggage. The implicit goal of their policies and their actions is not to defer to some outdated insistence on self-sufficiency, to buy off some well-wired constituency, to satisfy some emotional craving for the trappings of sovereignty, to tie up some bloc of votes, to feed some vocal demand for protection, or to keep some current government in power. It is to improve the quality of their people's lives by attracting and harnessing the talents and resources of the global economy, not by warding that economy off so that special interests can flourish.

No wonder, then, that when the people in Guangzhou tell their leaders in Beijing that they need to be joined with Hong Kong economically, if not politically, the latter's response is to say, Let's not get too carried away here. Let's not move too fast. Let's not create a model we might not want other regions to emulate. We want to control this. Greater openness may be necessary, but we want to decide when and how fast and how far. More to the point, we want to be sure that whatever new revenue such openness generates can be identified, captured, and put to use funding the civil minimums of less advanced areas. We have all of China to worry about, and we do worry. It is politically intolerable for us to let the economic fortunes of different regions get—and, worse, be seen to get—too far out of balance.

To which, naturally, the people in Guangzhou respond, You still don't get it. *You* may be worried about providing civil minimums, but *we* have to worry about how to become more like—as well as how to compete with—the Hong Kongs and Singapores and Taiwans of this world. We have to convince foreign investors that we are preferable to these other regions as a subject for their energies. They don't have to come here. They don't have to bring their money or their technology or their skills here. They can easily take them elsewhere. Press these golden geese too hard or make their laying house too unattractive, and they will work their magic in a competitor's backyard.

At the same time, of course, the people of Guangzhou know that they cannot deny a significant, ongoing relationship with the rest of mainland China. That connection is real—and is part of their strength and appeal. What they cannot afford is to be victims of tight, centralized control. But they can productively be—in fact, they would do well to be—part of a loose grouping of Chinese regional states, a kind of Chinese federation or commonwealth. This would well serve both sets of interests. The ironic lesson of history, however, is that when strong, centrally controlled nation states—the former Soviet Union, for example—prove unwilling to give up the illusion of power in order to enhance the quality of life of their people, the reality of that power erodes.

Old habits die hard, and the habits of power die hardest of all. Even—perhaps especially—when there has been a history of loose federation, as in the United States under the Articles of Confederation, there is often great reluctance to re-embrace either its logic or its ideals. All too often, what is remembered of those troubled years between the Treaty of Paris and the Constitution is the image of a feeble central government unable to do much of anything, let alone intervene effectively on the economic front. But it is precisely those protection-minded interventions that a return to federation is designed to prevent.

However soothing the illusion of control or of the beneficial effects of top-down intervention, the record shows that pitifully few such actions have ever restored hard-hit industries or regions to health. There are, of course, many kinds of policy actions by governments that *are* both useful and necessary. Just think, for example, of the financial regulation established during the early days of the New Deal in the U.S. But these are usually not the kinds of things that rabid defenders of central power have in mind.

Nation states, for the most part, opt for solutions that, however wasteful or inefficient, maintain at least the illusion of control. During the past ten years, for example, the United States has demanded more and more loudly that Japan open up its domestic market to rice.[5] The Rice Millers Association of America has played an influential lobbying role in Washington. After frustrating bilateral talks, the issue was brought into the Uruguay Round and, by extension, under the auspices of the new World Trade Organization. Japan has finally—and grudgingly—agreed to a gradual opening of its market, starting with 300,000 tons in 1993 and increasing by annual increments of 100,000 tons. In return, Japan will initially be able to assess a very stiff tariff, which will slowly decrease over time. This—as such nation state-based negotiations go—is a resounding victory.

However, what if Japan's 11 regional *do-shu* or natural business areas had been charged with handling the issue in place of the central government in Tokyo? The negotiators would have been the same people who have to compete with other *do-shus* for their economic survival, rather than those who face demands from local farmers and prefectural officials for more than US $10 billion a year in subsidies (*just to import rice worth only $300 million!*). Representatives from Tohoku-do, then, at the northeastern end of Honshu, might have chosen to visit rice-growing areas along the Mississippi in the United States and offer local farmers a deal: let us invest in your operations to produce high-quality and low-cost rice and then let us sell some percentage of it in Japan. U.S. farmers would then have had access to Japanese money and markets, and Tohoku-do farmers would have had access to a good business deal and to cheap rice for their people.

No one would fight to keep markets closed. Moreover, if all the *do-shus* behaved in a similar way and structured comparable deals with a variety of partners in Thailand, Australia, or wherever, Japanese consumers would stand to save more than US $40 billion annually from the grossly inflated prices they now have to pay. Everybody would win—except the lobbyists, who might find themselves out of a job. By contrast, leaving the issue to central governments means that Japanese farmers scream out against opening up the market and extort an additional US $72 billion from Tokyo to "permit" it, Japanese consumers have no access to inexpensive rice, and U.S. farmers have no access to Japanese money and only a tiny bit of access to their market. Everybody loses—except the lobbyists, who now enjoy even greater job security.

Because of the pressures operating on them, the predictable focus of nation states is on mechanisms for propping up troubled industries. This goes nowhere. The endless trade negotiations,[6] for example, between Japan and the United States, may have played well to voters back home, but the actions to which they led have rescued no industry, revived no sector of the economy, and been of advantage to no consumers. Textiles, semiconductors, automobiles, consumer electronics—these industries do not develop according to the whims of policymakers, but only in response to the defining logic of the competitive marketplace. If U.S. share in an industry has fallen, it is not because policy failed but because individual consumers decided to buy from other suppliers. But even when government policy succeeds—as, for example, did Japan's reluctant agreement to allow domestic sales of U.S.-made mobile phones—the home country does not benefit; the company does. In this case, the chips for the "U.S." handsets sold in Japan were made—and the handsets assembled—in Malaysia.

This, certainly, is not welcome news in established seats of power. Centrists shudder at the implications of region states or federations of region states because they have come to look upon the system of control they know best as if it were given in the very nature of things. But it is not. It is just an accident of history, nothing more, that modern economic theory crystallized at about the same time as the modern nation state. Had Adam Smith written one century earlier, it might be much easier for us now to view the connections between economic activity and nation states in quite a different light. So, too, if John Maynard Keynes had written half a century later. Indeed, for much of history, as Jane Jacobs reminds us in *Cities and the Wealth of Nations,* the meaningful units of economic life were—in fact, still are—urban aggregations and their respective hinterlands. It is centralized power over economic affairs that is the latecomer here. For a limited historical moment, it best suited the needs of development. That moment has now passed.

Where prosperity exists, it is region-based. And when a region prospers, its good fortune spills over into adjacent territories inside and outside the political federation of which it is a part. Economic progress in and around Bangkok, for example, has prompted investors to explore options elsewhere in Thailand. Much the same is true of Kuala Lumpur in Malaysia, of Jakarta in Indonesia, and, of course, of Singapore, which is rapidly becoming the unofficial capital of ASEAN. It could also be true of São Paulo in Brazil—if, that is, the central Brazilian government learns to treat it as a genuine region state and permits it to join the global economy. If it does, at least one region in Brazil could well join the OECD within ten years or so. If it does not—because of concerns for the civil minimum or fears that fairness among regions would be sacrificed—then the country as a whole may well fall off the roster of NIEs.

Region states are not—and need not be—the enemies of central government. Handled gently, by federation, these ports of entry to the global economy may well prove to be their very best friends.

Chapter Eight

ZEBRA STRATEGY

If you are selling ink-jet copiers, the product you develop for the dry climate of Arizona is probably not suitable for the damp and humid area around New Orleans. If you are selling gear for skiing, southern Germany is a lot more like Switzerland and other areas along the Upper Rhine than it is like Hamburg. If you are selling home furniture, wouldn't you rather the island of Kyushu be linked directly with Pusan in Korea, with its 4.5 million people and only 25-minute distance away by plane, rather than with a Japan country manager based in Tokyo, who will "average" Kyushu data so that it all sounds Tokyo-like before reporting it back to headquarters in New York or London or Rome? (In fact, 20 percent of the people on Kyushu who buy furniture for their new homes already buy it from Taiwan or Korea.) If you are selling sneakers for outdoor use in winter, wouldn't it make more sense for you to bundle Milwaukee with Toronto than with Dallas?

Whatever you are selling in a borderless economy, it is better to do it *not* through a U.N.-style amalgam of nation-based organizations, but through a region state-focused network of capability and competence. After all, the acid test for region states is not whether they sound nice in theory or whether the hype surrounding them has reached fever pitch. It is whether real managers in real companies with real dollars to invest and real commitments to make act in a fashion consistent with their existence—and their importance.

Fifteen years ago, even ten years ago, they did not. Their view, at the time, of how best to arrange the international activities of their companies was based, implicitly, on a United Nations-style view of the world. Each country had a place at the economic table, and each place at the table had a name card with an individual country's name. Back then, as a manager, if you decided to go into France, you went into France—not Burgundy or Provence or Auvergne, but France—and once there, you set up a French clone of the organization you had already built in Germany or the U.K. or wherever. Even if your activities actually covered—and were intended to cover—only a fraction of that nation's geography, your strategy was still a country strategy, and the organization you built was a country organization.

Today, by contrast, what does it mean for a company to go into China? With an office or two in Guangdong, is it possible to "cover" the country or even to delude yourself that you are doing so? Is covering the country, in fact, what you should really be aspiring to do? There are vast disparities of wealth from region to region (see Exhibit 8–1), some of which have per capita GDPs greater than those of many freestanding Asian countries (see Exhibit 8–2). The disparities are equally great from city to city within a region (see Exhibit 8–3).

Moreover, given the limited state of transportation and communications infrastructure, you would do well to be able to cover a few parts of just Guangdong itself, which has more than 60 million people and 20 fair-sized, autonomous cities. Add to that both the 20 million overseas Chinese who think of Guangdong as home and the neighboring population of Hong Kong, which is part of the coastal area's region state, and the resulting population of 85 million or so is roughly equivalent to that of the largest European economy, the reunified Germany.

The only reasonable approach, therefore, is to plan a strategy and build an organization for Guangdong alone, but to do so in ways that are "plug-compatible"—that is, that permit useful, working linkages to be formed—with what you are now doing or may in the future decide to do in the 27 other, Beijing-designated, "official" regions of the country. This, of course, is what U.S. firms have done for years as they

EXHIBIT 8–1

GDP Per Capita in China, 1991

(US $)

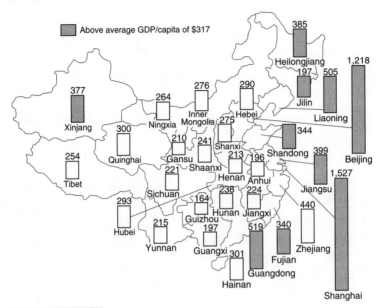

Note: Average official exchange rate for 1991 is 5.51 Yuan per US$.

Source: China Statistical Yearbook 1993.

moved into the European market. They did not "enter" Europe by trying to build an integrated, continent-wide operation with a single European headquarters at Brussels or Amsterdam. They went country by country. Only in recent years, as coordination problems among these separate operations have grown and as the economic geography of a true European Union has come, at last, closer to reality, are they moving to construct the institutional basis for a genuine, pan-European presence.

Thus, with China today as with Europe a generation or two ago, the real choice managers face is not whether to enter, but which region(s) to enter. But the opportunity to tie their decision to regional, rather than national, considerations is, if anything, greater than it was in the early, heady days of European expansion. The game is different now because the intervening years have witnessed the rapid evolution of a global economy. As a result, local clusters of activity do not need to look, in the first instance, for "external" markets, partners in trade,

EXHIBIT 8–2

GNP Ranking of Japanese *Do-Shu*
(*US $ billions*)

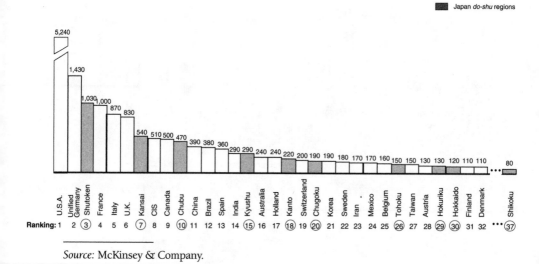

Japan *do-shu* regions

Source: McKinsey & Company.

technical and managerial skills, or sources of capital in neighboring areas within the same nation state. They can look, instead, to strike arrangements with economic actors anywhere in the world.

Beijing, for instance, has agreed to permit the nation's official regions—each an "island of opportunity" in its own right—to negotiate independently with foreign providers of capital and infrastructure-related expertise. Why, then, build costly telecom networks to send messages to a sparsely populated interior when you can put a satellite dish on the roof, bounce signals off the heavens, and communicate directly with London and New York and Tokyo?

Even local developments in China are now global in orientation. Xu Kuangdi, for example, the former professor of metallurgy who is now executive vice-mayor of Shanghai, leads the committee that oversees all new infrastructure projects in both Shanghai and Pudong, the city's special economic development zone. By late 1994, the committee's expenditure on roads, bridges, tunnels, and the like came to more than US $6 billion. But that's just a beginning. By the end of the decade, the committee plans to harness the efforts of foreign partners to invest more than $100 billion in such projects. Helping Xu in these

EXHIBIT 8–3

Per Capita GDP by City, 1992–2000
(US $)

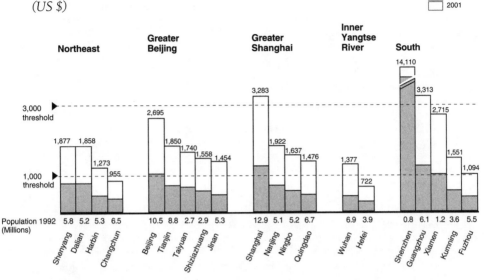

Note: Figures have been projected using 9.1% Chinese CAGR for 1985–92.
Source: China Statistical Yearbook 1993; McKinsey estimates; T.17.8.

efforts is the old boys' network of former Shanghai officials, including Chiang Zeming and Zhu Rongji, who now manage the country's vast but fragile economy.

For global managers, the bright, attractive—and manageable—spots on today's development maps are not countries but bounded regions like Shanghai/Pudong, which are appealing in themselves as a market, as a base from which to provide both manufactured goods and services, and as a functioning link to the borderless economy. Shanghai with its hinterland, including the neighboring provinces of Jiangsu and Zhejiang, has a total population of some 125 million—roughly equal to all of Japan. Thus, a monolithic strategy for "entering Greater Shanghai" is almost as nonsensical as one for "entering Japan." A foothold in the Pudong region might be reasonable, however, as might a beachhead in the Kansai area around Osaka. But trying to swallow a difficult new market of 125 million people all in one convulsive gulp is not.

Much the same is true, of course, of India. Entering the regions centered on Bombay or Madras or Bangalore is a plausible managerial task. Entering "India" is not. So, too, with Jakarta in Indonesia. And so, too, with northern California or the Pacific Northwest or New England in the United States. Up close and on the ground, the managerial tasks of building a business in any one of these areas are substantially different from those in another. From a great distance, however, there is an overwhelming impulse to generalize and lump together. I no longer bother to count the times a European or American executive calls me in Tokyo to see if we can get together while he is visiting "my region." Translated, what this really means is that he intends to fly to Sydney or Jakarta, which are eight or nine hours from Tokyo by air.

In one such conversation, a manager told me that he had lined up three professionals in Beijing, none a Mandarin speaker, and several "qualified salesmen," who had been identified through a newspaper ad, to launch a building materials business in China. True, he was a little sheepish about the "qualifying" process, but felt reasonably good about the morale of the group and about the ambitiousness of their initial proposals. There was absolutely no awareness on his part that his plans were the logical equivalent of sticking three French speakers in Washington, D.C., in order to sell bricks all across the United States. Or that, even if he were able to hire suitable Mandarin speakers, the differences among Chinese dialects are so huge as to make them mutually unintelligible. Conditioned to think only in terms of nation states, he had no ready way to see that the geographical reach of his country-based planning was at an entirely wrong—an impossible—level of scale. He should have been looking at regions instead.

Regions matter, in part, because the scale of effort they imply is managerially doable. But they also matter because they so readily lend themselves as ports of entry to the global economy. None of the regions now flourishing or beginning to flourish has gotten that way by circling its wagons around a protected base of natural resources, dribbling those resources out to clamorous buyers at artificially maintained prices, and then passing their revenues on to a central government eager to fund the civil minimum elsewhere. This is certainly not what Shanghai is doing. It is certainly not what Singapore or Silicon Valley or Wales or Penang or Catalonia has done.

The lesson is painfully clear, but in many quarters there is often great reluctance to accept it. National governments still tend to view unequal rates or patterns of growth across regions as destabilizing problems to be solved rather than as opportunities to be harnessed. They worry not about how to help successful areas prosper further, but about how best to extract money from them so as to fund the civil minimum. They worry about the adequacy of their policy instruments for controlling clusters of economic activity on radically different trajectories of growth. And they worry about protecting those activities from the distorting effects of transborder flows of information and capital and expertise.

These are the wrong kinds of things to worry about. They have to do primarily with maintaining centralized control, even at the expense of dragging all parts of the country down. They do not have to do with letting individual regions flourish and so provide the energy, stimulus, and support to bring the rest along. Multinational corporations (MNCs) can read these signals with perfect clarity, and they stay away.

In the former Soviet Union, for example, the race is on to see whether it is possible to arrest and reverse the damage done by years of such heavy-handed central control to natural economic regions like Baku, the capital of Azerbaijan, or Irkutsk, Nakhodka, Khabarovsk, and Vladivostok in Siberia. If allowed to create their own linkages with the global economy and to strike their own deals with the managers of global enterprises, each of these regions may still prosper and so give Moscow one less problem to worry about. But if such permission is denied, the global economy will be scared away. The managers of MNCs will, quite understandably, focus their attention elsewhere and leave these regions to inescapable decay.

THE ZEBRA'S STRIPES

The economies of nation states are not monolithic. In the real world, remember, there is no such thing as an "average" Italy or France or Japan or United States. For managers, such averages are useless statistical abstractions—and misleading abstractions at that. They seem to imply that it is meaningful, even desirable, to make critical decisions about strategy and investment on a country-by-country basis. Yes, the

American market is large and growing; let's enter. No, the risk of operating in Thailand makes us uncomfortable; let's wait. This is nonsense.

I do not mean that there are no relevant differences in policy, regulatory, legal, or general market environment from country to country. Of course there are, and MNC managers must pay attention to them. My point is that the vast majority of the real, hands-on decisions that these managers confront have to be made at an entirely different level of granularity.

The Japanese companies with which I have worked for years have never devised strategies or built organizations to enter the U.S. market as a whole, as if it were a single unified area. It isn't, and they knew better. Instead, they would pick and choose their spots: California, perhaps, and maybe New England, the Great Lakes area, and, at least initially, very little else. Although, from a distance, the whole of the United States might look gray, they understood that the markets for their products were not evenly distributed, coast to coast; there were pockets of intense interest here and there with great swatches of "white space" between.

They also understood that the isobars of demand on the U.S. consumer map varied significantly from product to product. Consumer taste in clothing or automobile accessories might be relatively constant throughout California, north to south, but might vary considerably when it came to packaged foods or consumer electronics. And even when overall growth rates in a single product market were at X percent, some parts of the country would be booming along at X+Y and others lagging behind at X-Z. The inevitable result: strategy maps that, when seen up close, looked like the hide of a zebra—not gray, but darkly shaded areas of activity separated by white space.

In economic terms, at the level of granularity relevant to managers, all nation states are zebras. Media vary, growth rates vary, infrastructure varies, tastes and preferences vary. There is information-driven convergence, to be sure, but it does not proceed everywhere at an equal pace. Indeed, part of what makes region states such attractive economic units is the fact that—along these axes—their internal variance is far less than that between them and other regions in a zebra-striped economy. Though linked by common adherence to the same center-defined macroeconomic policies, such regions may have relatively little in common. Around their immediate periphery, however, there is often a steadily expanding "gray" hinterland, which shares their particular mix of attitudes and tastes, if in reduced degree, through a kind of spillover effect.

If you, a manager, sit in Bangkok, you may not be able to "see" with great clarity all that is going on elsewhere in Thailand. The differences are too great. Chiang Mai and Chiang Rai, both in the northern mountains, have quite a different culture from that of, say, Phuket, off the southwest coast. But you may be able to "see" what is going on in the *baht*-defined zone of influence, spreading out from Bangkok, that runs across the border to Laos, Cambodia, and even Myanmar and Vietnam. U.N.-style, nation state-focused policy may be intentionally blind to these developments: Myanmar, after all, is off limits, and Cambodia is deeply suspect. But Thai Air has a regular flight to Rangoon, informal trade moves continuously across the Salween River between Thailand and Myanmar, and sundry business dealings with Khymer interests are far more real and tangible than the distant pronouncements, to which the West listens so closely, of President Sihanouk from his residence in Beijing.

In much the same fashion, if you sit in Tokyo or Osaka, you will have, at best, an arm's-length view of developments in China. That is why a company like Sanyo has relocated its first executive vice president from Osaka to Dalian. He can see northeastern China much better from there. Similarly, if you sit in Singapore or Kuala Lumpur, with their mixture of ethnic Malays, Chinese, and Indians, you are at the de facto center of a hub-and-spoke communications network joining several of the largest economies in the world. You are, in effect, at a crossroads of information—much as you would have been a generation ago if you had set up an eastern bloc "listening post" in Vienna or Helsinki. These spots might not make ideal operational centers, but they have immense value as a region-spanning perch from which to lay out strategy and develop people.

In the past, you might have been attracted to these locations by their low rates of taxation or by their proximity to raw materials or cheap labor. Today, the attraction is increasingly the intimacy of their knowledge- and culture-rooted connection with several of the most appealing regions of growth in the world. The white spaces in between do not matter. Perhaps, for Triad-based decision makers, the risks in Myanmar or Cambodia or the noncoastal parts of China may simply be too distant to see and assess directly. But there will be Thai or Malaysian or Singaporean partners and middlemen who can. And who consistently do. Hunan Air has regular flights to Bangkok. From Kuala Lumpur to Bombay it is less than four hours. And there are 25 shuttle flights daily between Singapore and Kuala Lumpur operated jointly by MAS and SIA. Believe it or not, *these* are the most frequent cross-border flights in the entire world.

EQUIDISTANCE

Zebras exist. Their most active stripes—and the gray hinterlands surrounding them—often fall across the borders of nation states. This creates no end of problems for MNCs. In the organizations that most now have in place, there is room for corporate headquarters, regional headquarters, and country-level management, as well as crosscutting worldwide product divisions. Adding to this mix a separate structure for the major region states—of which there may now be 30 or so to which a typical MNC would want to pay attention—would boost the number of organizational levels, which most MNCs have been trying to cut down for years.

But even if this renewed complexity were deemed worthwhile, adding a level would not fix matters, because the economic realities of region states would still not be clearly visible to managers at the center. No matter how noble their intentions, the intervening layer of country management would, inevitably, filter the data and average it. Experience shows that this is not the way for global CEOs to become genuinely "equidistant" in their thinking from all the places in which their companies operate.

Nor, however, can the problem be solved by having region states report in directly to the group at the center. The resulting span of control would be much too big. Worse still, while nation states have clear borders, region states do not. The solid lines that surround countries also circumscribe relatively discrete bodies of data on flows of information, trade, capital, people, and the like. True, most conventional statistics about these flows are deeply flawed, but able country management teams know how to create numbers that do reflect real levels and patterns of activity. For region states, however, whose borders do not follow the clear lines of Euclidean geometry but the blurred dots and splotches of an Impressionist painting, building accurate data is a far harder task.

Region states are not neat boxes into which neat sets of facts can be packed. They are, instead, much more like magnets hovering over a field of moving metal scraps, bending and twisting the flows as they go.

The usual organizational solutions, therefore, do not work. Something else is needed. One possibility is to stay with a country manager system, but support it with an information system geared to these regional flows of activity. Another is to create, across a whole region like Asia-Pacific, a nonsymmetrical matrix. Country organizations and their attendant information systems would remain where the critical need is to deal with central governments on policy matters (airline privatization, for example, or telecoms policy), but the rest would be organized, horizontally across nation states, by issue: procurement, R&D, information technology, and so on. Especially where the business in question is information-intensive, the horizontal cut by issue holds the greatest promise for ensuring equidistance.

Think, for example, of an engineering business based in Singapore, but relying on product design and programming skills in India, design integration in Kuala Lumpur, financial services in Hong Kong, outsourced manufacturing in several regions of China driven by workstations in Bangalore and Kuala Lumpur, component assembly in Penang, and sales in the United States. The company's work is not an aggregation of country-level activities, but a disaggregated business system run as a networked process, controlled by shared information, and organized horizontally by issue.

This is not some improbable, futuristic vision. I am working with half a dozen leading companies in Asia-Pacific that are doing precisely this kind of thing right now. Even their most intensely "local" activities, like customer satisfaction, can be delivered locally but managed from elsewhere as part of the network. With the appropriate database, IT systems, and communications in place, for instance, there is no reason why Japanese-speaking customer service representatives cannot sit in Hong Kong or Singapore or wherever the telecom bills are the cheapest and take care of the needs of the 600,000 Japanese businessmen working around the world outside Japan.

MNCs, therefore, no longer need to build a series of U.N.-style clone organizations, country by country, which they then oversee from the great distance of some corporate Mount Olympus.[1] Such organizations are cumbersome, at best, and they tend to miss or filter out the realities of region states. Instead, for most purposes, MNCs can create a horizontal network, the nodes of which—equidistant from the center—are not arbitrary geographical units but real issue- or area-based flows of economic activity, many of which involve participation by external partners and vendors. Again, the creation of such borderless companies for a borderless world is not armchair theorizing. It is already happening.

One of the prime difficulties of organizing a company for global operations is the psychology of managers who are used to thinking by country-based line of authority rather than by line of opportunity. Lots of creative ideas for generating value are overlooked because such managers are captive to nation state-conditioned habits of mind. Once that constraint is relaxed and those habits are broken, however, a nearly infinite range of new opportunities comes into focus: building cross-border alliances or joint ventures, establishing virtual companies, arbitraging differential costs of labor or even services (postage, say, or utilities or phone bills). In fact, given the potential to redesign business systems implicit in today's information technology and Internet-like networks, regional "solutions" will be increasingly powerful tools for outflanking the competition. I strongly believe that, as head-to-head battles within established geographies yield less and less incremental value, changing the battleground from nation to cross-border region will be at the core of 21st-century corporate strategy.

This kind of shift in focus has to happen. A leading Western consumer product firm has long organized for its global markets by moving virtually all production out of its home country and into manufacturing "hubs" in Asia and Latin America, which then coordinate networks of operations throughout the neighboring region. Its Mount Olympus-like headquarters remains in the home country, where all the functional and worldwide product division heads are also located.

The firm's regional headquarters for Asia-Pacific, which is in Hong Kong, has all of the region's country-based national sales companies reporting to it. The only task for these companies is execution. All key elements of strategy—product planning, design, local variations—are decided somewhere back on the home mountain. When there are differences in opinion between in-country and home mountain dwellers, the former have a very hard time being taken seriously. Because the staff at the center are so expert and experienced, the lack of sophistication at the country level makes opinions from the periphery relatively easy to ignore or discredit.

When the Olympians were finally convinced that they had to substantially boost the mix of skills in each country market, their initial impulse was to replicate the full mix of Olympus-style capabilities at the various regional headquarters and then to add some more capability at the country level as needed. The inevitable result: more—and more elaborate—organizational levels, a head count explosion, and a dramatic rise in SG&A costs. When even these arrangements did not boost local performance, the only remaining choice was to remove a country's management team and replace it.

At the same time, however, the long-established business system of the industry in which the company participated was coming unglued. Leveraging new information technology, players in the industry's retail channel quickly gained strength. Able to identify the best and cheapest sources of product from around the globe, they could now arbitrage product opportunities wherever they exist. A Florida-based automobile tire distributor, for instance, could find and source good quality tires made in China for US $12 and then make them available—at only a tiny markup—to a retailer in Kyushu. Even with transaction and logistics costs added in, this is a great deal: Japanese producers cannot even get their hands on the raw material needed to make a tire for US $12.

In such a globally linked environment, being the proud owner of an expensive, multilayer, country-focused corporate organization is, at best, a recipe for stagnation. If a French customer can get a better price for your product by sourcing it through a discount distributor based in the U.K., thereby bypassing your multiple levels of cost, you—as country manager for France—are plain out of luck. Put simply, when such cross-border arbitrage is possible, the only arrangement that makes sense is to run your operation, in effect, as a "virtual" company—that is, as a flat, networked organization with a disaggregated ability to manage an ever-shifting network of functions and services.

Conventional wisdom has it that the sales function, for example, is so intensely local in nature that it makes no sense—in fact, it is highly counterproductive—to organize it in any other way than as a series of local activity clusters. But, for many consumer products, if you have access to information about potential customers around the world, you can build a sales operation to reach them that has virtually no local presence. You can print catalogues and price lists wherever you want and make them available by mail, phone, fax, or personal computer (through Internet). Then, since it is likely that most people in the markets you want to reach have credit cards, which are attached to one or another form of international payment clearing system, your customers can place their order—again, by phone, fax, mail, or personal computer—charge it to their credit card, and have it delivered through a global parcel service like Federal Express or UPS. The result: equidistant local service, but no local presence.

Much the same is true of manufacturing. By dint of sharing groupware, databases, and dedicated private networks, there is no need for a company's manufacturing locations to be sited near its engineering center. The relevant information can be transferred, in real time, from anywhere to anywhere around the world. Equally important, today's sophisticated machine tools, assembly machines, insertion machines, and the like are "smart" enough that they can be run from regular PCs or workstations using the appropriate software, not just from unit-specific controllers. That means it is now possible to set up in China, using local workers trained on new workstations, a world-class operation for making VCR cylinder heads. By contrast, it would have been strictly impossible ten, or even five, years ago to transfer such quality-sensitive operations, which require submicron accuracy, from the highly skilled workers of Germany and Japan to their less well-trained counterparts in the United States or ASEAN.

Furthermore, since the real value added in such operations comes from the "intelligence" embedded in the design, fabrication, and assembly instructions shared by these machines, running the network means staying equidistantly informed about those firms that, no matter where they are located, are able to supply relevant components in the right places, at the right times, at the right level of quality, and at the right price. Manufacturing management is no longer a task of bending metal and joining things together in one or another nation state, but of overseeing a horizontal, global network of information.

Thus, the management challenge represented jointly by the emergence of region states and the availability of new, information-driven enabling technologies is not most effectively met through country units, even when set in a matrix with worldwide product units. These two new realities have combined to change what it is that a corporate organization needs to be in a genuinely borderless world.

No longer is the goal to build a mini-U.N. of nation state-based operating units. Nor is it to build a product-focused structure that cuts across these U.N.-style divides. Instead, as much of the best new thinking on strategy has it, it is to create and oversee a global network of disaggregated skills, competencies, and capabilities—some of which get bundled with the products and services normally available for sale and some of which get sold as products or services in their own right. In strategic terms, of course, this represents a disaggregation of—and a recombination among—the discrete elements of the familiar business system in and across industries. But it also represents the core logic on which organizations fit for a world of region states— those magnets shaping and skewing the flow of economic activity— must be built.

In the past, MNCs were willing to accept the burden of an additional hierarchical level—the country manager—in order to get the benefit of dealing effectively with unevenness across markets. They do not need to make that trade-off any longer. Country managers, remember, may be needed to deal with local government leaders on policy questions, but they do not represent real markets. By definition, clusters of taste and preference, together with meaningful economies of service (advertising "reach," TV channel "reach," distribution costs, and the like), exist instead at the region state level. People in Vancouver watch Seattle TV channels; people in Guangdong, Hong Kong channels. Only from a distance does a zebra seem gray. Up close, its various regions have a life and a character of their own.

Chapter Nine

THE NATION STATE'S RESPONSE

When the Secretary General of the United Nations calls the General Assembly to order, the delegates in the chamber—all 184 of them—each have a single vote in the assembly's deliberations. They represent nation states ranging in size from China, with its 1.2 billion people, and Russia, with its 6.5 million square miles of territory stretching across 11 time zones, to Nauru, with not quite 8,000 people on an island atoll barely eight square miles in extent. Major world economies are not directly represented—chief among them, of course, being Taiwan and Hong Kong. The region around Tokyo, the third largest economy in the world (not counting Japan itself), is there only by proxy. So is California. So is Catalonia. Major peoples are not directly represented—the Kurds, for example, and the Zulu and Palestinians. And major clusters of interest are not directly represented—NAFTA, say, and the EU, and APEC.

Because the only entities officially "visible" to the U.N. are traditional nation states, when their delegates announce, with the kind of smug modesty entirely suitable to sound-bite news coverage, that "all is quiet on the Western front," there is no choice but to honor their verdict—unless, of course, there are questions about the rule book legitimacy of the governments that sent them. In practice, this means that issues not falling into the neat box of country versus country usu-

117

ally cannot get on the U.N.'s agenda until they have reached such catastrophic proportions—a famine, a massacre, a plague, a pattern of genocide—that even international bureaucrats can no longer avert their gaze.

Increasingly, the circumstances requiring the attention of the world community do not conveniently follow the borders of nation states or the remit of the multilateral or global institutions that bridge them. They are, for the most part, problems having to do not with *realpolitik* or the balance of power, but with the daily lives—and the daily quality of life—of ordinary people in ordinary settings. The lens associated with nation states tends to filter such problems out. As a practical matter, people do not live and work in countries. Day to day, their relevant sphere of life is local or regional.

As the locus of economic activity, countries, after all, are zebras. Western Australia, for example, has growing linkages with Singapore and Indonesia; New South Wales with Hong Kong and Taiwan; Queensland with Japan; and Victoria, especially Melbourne, with Greece. The percentage of the population of New South Wales that is of Asian descent is now well into the double digits, and there are daily flights from six different Japanese airports to Australia's east coast. Similarly, except for power generation, telecoms, and airlines, the 27 separate regions of China are largely free to go their own way, according to the regional authorities, in developing their industrial base with whatever foreign participation they can—or choose to—attract. For the most part, the southern regions have focused on petrochemicals and processed foods; the areas around the Yellow Sea, like Dalian and Tianjin, on electronics.

There is no way that China, as a single nation state, could pull in the necessary resources from MNCs, multilateral lending agencies, or the taxation of its own citizens. Nor is there any way that it could either fund or manage the needed levels, countrywide, of infrastructure development on its own. As a federation of separate, deal-making regions, however, it can—and is. A region-specific BOT (build–operate–transfer) scheme, for instance, is already harnessing foreign resources and skills to build a critical highway from Shenzhen to Guangzhou and the Three Gorges dam along the Yangtze River Chang Jiang.

Inviting in private foreign capital to help build infrastructure, as China is doing, is an idea now being seriously considered by countries like the Philippines, Vietnam, and India. In the past, infrastructure building was a largely "sovereign" activity. If the central government of a developing country needed financial assistance, it turned to the World Bank or to development credits from more advanced countries. This was the kind of arrangement that central governments made among themselves—or with a very small number of multilateral agencies. There was some discipline exerted on government, but not much. The trans-Guangdong highway, however, is being built privately by Hopewell, led by Gordon Wu of Hong Kong, in return for the carefully bounded privilege of keeping all toll revenues for a specific number of years. Because the global economy has been invited in, real discipline gets exerted and everyone benefits: investors, taxpayers (whose money is freed up for other uses), and those who will use the road once it is finished.

ZONES OF INCLUSION

The temptation for old-fashioned government policymakers is to view such a disaggregation of effort as a necessary evil that has to be tolerated. To some extent, this is an entirely predictable response to the loss of control by people used to control—or, at least, to the illusion of control. But it also reflects their suspicion about the true ends toward which such centrifugal forces are being directed.

It is one thing for factional leaders in Northern Ireland, say, to call for independence as a means of ensuring less cumbersome linkages with the global economy. But it is quite another if their underlying motive is to use that greater independence to drive through their own, highly sectarian agendas. Regional autonomy is a great—an essential—lever for taking advantage of the global economy to the benefit of all citizens and residents. But it can also be used as a plausible and public rationale, under the cover of which religious, racial, ethnic, or tribal groups privately aspire to advance only their own, self-interested ends.

These are legitimate concerns. Effective region states are inclusive. Their scale makes inclusion easier. They welcome anyone who contributes. And they welcome any contribution, foreign or domestic, that adds to the common good. They need everyone's help for economic success. Unfortunately, however, the historical record is littered with regions as well as nations that ignored their shared economic interests and succumbed, instead, to the passions of ethnicity, religion, race, and tribe.

There is, then, no sure guarantee that regions will be inclusive. And there will always be those at the center who point to that uncertainty as justification for maintaining tight control of economic and social policy at the national level. In the United States, they will point out that it was legislation coming out of Washington and not the states that, 100 years after the end of the Civil War, finally brought some measure of social justice and economic opportunity to Southern blacks. This is true as far as it goes, but it does not go far enough. Washington-based action did, indeed, put the laws on the books. But it was the locally driven, ground-level, day-to-day economic reality of a growing Southern economy that provided the wherewithal to make them real.

Nation states and their governments do, of course, have a vital interest in propagating and enforcing the values of inclusiveness that hold their societies together. But, especially in today's borderless economy, it is the economic engine of region states that ties these abstract concepts to very tangible pocketbooks and embeds them in the quality of the lives people actually lead.

FROM MALAY DILEMMA TO MALAY DELIGHT

In this context, review with me the successes to date of Malaysia's "Look East" strategy of economic development.[1] Prior to 1980, Malaysia was primarily an exporter of commodity raw materials, and its fortunes fluctuated wildly up and down with each change in the prices of those commodities, over which the government had little if any control. As a small country—with a population then of only 13 million or so—there was little it could do to improve its fortunes, across the board, by investing heavily in the full range of manufacturing industries.

Wisely, under the leadership of Prime Minister Mahathir, Malaysia opted instead to focus on building world-class "vertical" capabilities in just a few industries: semiconductors, automobiles, and consumer packaged goods. Moreover, it did so with the full expectation that its long-term advantage—given the likely emergence of India, China, and other extremely low-wage Asian nations—did not lie in its currently low labor costs but, rather, in its potential mastery of each industry's full value-added chain. Malaysia would not just assemble semiconductors; it would also learn to do wafer fabrication. It would not just assemble automobiles; it would manufacture components as well.

This strategy, brilliantly executed against competitor nations at roughly the same level of development, such as Indonesia and the Philippines, has now brought the country to an average GNP per capita of US $3,000. But getting from there to, say, US $5,000 by the end of the decade will be a much harder task. A good portion of the growth to date has been the direct result of the effectiveness with which "inputs" like capital and an educated work force have been brought to bear in a systematic fashion on carefully selected economic priorities. It is simply not possible to repeat these effects, at the same order of magnitude, forever.

Equally important, the identity of competitor nations has changed and, with it, the nature of competition. In economic terms, China and India are, at last, emerging on the world scene and both have far larger populations, much smaller (and, thus, capable of much faster growth) per capita GNPs, and much lower labor costs. In the Chinese city of Dalian, for example, great numbers of talented electronics factory workers are available at only one seventh of the Malaysian wage.

In this kind of changed environment, a strategy based on traditional, labor-based, manufacturing value-added is no longer enough. It should not be prematurely abandoned, but it is not likely to be endlessly sustainable. As a result, Malaysia will have to find an innovative new way to build on its strengths. It does not have to worry about its small size. If its strategy makes sense, the whole world will be its market. Nor does it have to worry about having enough money or the right technology. Again, if its strategy is right, the global economy will provide them.

All Malaysia has to worry about is properly defining a strategy that leverages its strengths as a centrally placed, successfully multiracial society in a region that will, by the turn of the century, be home to four or five of the ten largest economies in the world. This means it must find a way to effect the transition from manufacturing- to knowledge-based value added—and it must do so in a fashion that distinctively positions it as providing the core hub-and-spokes of the Asia-Pacific region's rapidly developing information economy.[2]

Malaysia can, for example, follow Singapore's lead and deepen its ties with software-based, high-tech industries in India. It actually has an advantage here in that it has among its population ten times more ethnic Indians than Singapore does. Again, like Singapore, it can deepen its ties with knowledge-intensive industries in China—and, again, it has a people-based advantage: twice the number of ethnic Chinese that Singapore has. And it can forge comparable links with Indonesia because communication between the two countries is relatively easy in the Malay language.

No other country in the world sits so comfortably in the middle of—or is so well placed to communicate with—these three giant economies. Meanwhile, the focus of the past decade's "Look East" program has deeply familiarized the Malaysian people with the economic policies and management styles of Japan and Korea. Equally important, as the most industrially advanced Islamic nation in the world, Malaysia has a special opportunity to play a central role in helping other Islamic nations integrate with the global economy. Its potential network of knowledge-based influence in rapidly growing parts of the world is thus both extensive and unique.

At the conceptual level, the attractiveness of this strategy is clear. What makes it practical, however, is Malaysia's balanced success as a multiracial society—that is, its theory and practice of inclusion. It still, to be sure, has many of its own internal development needs to address. And in addressing them it must make sure that, in addition to Kuala Lumpur and Penang, region states like Johore have whatever communications infrastructure they will need to participate actively in these cross-border networks. These, however, are resources for strategy implementation. What enables that strategy in the first place is Malaysia's self-fulfilling vision as a zone of inclusion.

Reflecting on the accomplishments of his "Look East" policy, Prime Minister Mahathir recently told me that the secret to its success was

time. Unlike many Western and virtually all Japanese leaders, Dr. Mahathir has been at the helm for 13 years—a goodly stretch, but still far
shorter than Lee Kwan Yew's 30-year tenure as prime minister of Singapore. In this context, Exhibit 9–1, which shows Malaysia's per capita GNP during Dr. Mahathir's term of office, is quite revealing. If he
had left office in, say, year five, in 1986, there would have been very
little to show for all his talk about building an automobile and semiconductor industry. All significant economic changes take time to re-
alize their effects, and there is often a short-term dip in performance
along the road to long-term prosperity. How many nation states, given
the power of their vested interest groups, have the ability to stay the
course?

A ROLE FOR THE CENTER

At home, in Japan, I have proposed that the nation state be divided,
for economic purposes, into 11 independent *do-shu,* or regions, so
that the rest of the country can make a connection with the global
economy free of the distorting and controlling influence of the bureaucrats and politicians in Tokyo. By itself, the island of Kyushu, remember, has an economy larger than that of Korea, Holland, Mexico,
or Australia; Kansai, the region around Osaka, an economy larger than

EXHIBIT 9–1

Malaysian per Capita GNP

(US $)

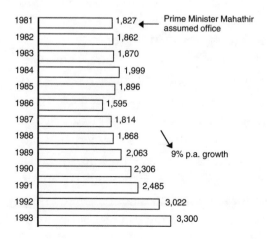

that of Russia, Spain, or Canada as previously shown in Exhibit 8–2. But neither of them will—or can—develop sound policies or a self-sufficient industrial base until the lion's share of the income it receives stops coming, by way of redistribution, from the central government in Tokyo.

This kind of planned economy—the working basis for the much discussed "Japan, Inc."—may have made sense at an earlier stage of the country's development. But now, with the yen so expensive and with the competitive fortunes of its various industries so widely dispersed, continued direction from the center can mean only ever-greater subsidies to the areas and industries left behind.

Politically, however, redistribution is an addictive process. It does work, powerfully so. It does buy votes. But the more it works, the greater the appetite is for it to continue at higher and higher levels. Under a democratic form of government, this process can reach a point of no return, beyond which a subsidized and civil minimum-ed majority will have neither the need nor the incentive to allow a more sustainable balance to be struck.

Having established undisputed ownership and title to the golden goose, such a majority is not about to let it slip from its grasp. It may be convinced to relax its grip when confronted, say, by the kind of economic paralysis that results when GNP becomes more than 75 percent dominated by the government sector, as in Sweden. But there is no guarantee even then. Aomori City—with its annual budget of US $1.8 billion on a local tax base of US $300 million—has gotten used to its indoor baseball stadiums and public swimming pools and miles of paved highway on which virtually no one travels.

When local governments are so generously provided for, they rarely take the initiative to build an industrial base for the future. Why bother? Why make the effort? The money, after all, will come in one way or another. Over time, however, this flow of resources leads not to a strengthening of the local economic base but to a thoroughly dependent, consumption-oriented society. Moreover, it is a society that progressively organizes itself around this easy money into a nearly feudal, patronage-based hierarchy of local officials, mayors, and governors. This dependency on public sector handouts does not remain constant over time: it grows worse. The longer autonomy and responsibility for

EXHIBIT 9–2

An Example of Japan's Local Economty

(1994)

	Aomori Prefecture			Aomori City*		
Population	1,507,037			296,939		
Annual budget at $1 = ¥100	$7,558 million			$1,858 million		
Number of employees	6,500 (at the prefectural government)			3,287 (at the municipal government)		
Largest private companies	Industry	Sales	Number of employees	Industry	Sales	Number of employees
		$ Millions			$ Millions	
	1. Steel wholesale	1,027	791	1. Wholesale	386	522
				2. Pachinko	379	864
	2. Local bank	878	1,853	3. Department store	382	580
	3. Local bank	877	1,890			
	4. Alcohol wholesale	461	460	4. Newspaper	128	485
			742	5. Bakery	87	720
	5. Consumer electronics	261				
		3,594	5,736		1,362	3,171

*Capital of Aomori Prefecture.

the future are delayed, the more deeply rooted the addiction becomes. Today, for precisely this reason, more than 90 percent of Japan's local townships and cities face a bleak economic future: they have lost all independent willpower—save the urge to feed their addiction.

Look, for a moment, at Exhibit 9–2, which sketches the fairly typical economic situation of Aomori City and Aomori Prefecture in 1994. Note, first, that the prefecture's annual budget is much larger than the combined turnover of the top five local companies. Much the same is true of its roster of employees. The public sector is the only growth industry there. Except for the local subsidiary of a large Japanese consumer electronics company, the vast majority of nonpublic-sector workers are in service-related industries, not manufacturing. In Aomori City itself, on the manufacturing side, there is a *miso* (fermented bean) producer with US $67 million in sales and 254 employees, and a fish cannery with US $53 million and 182 people—and not much else. Even so, Aomori City has aspirations to get on the global map: it is, for example, a candidate to host the 2002 World Cup soccer event. But its plans do not rest on building a vibrant local industrial base linked with the rest of the world. They rest, instead, on the assumption that the central government will continue to drop into the city's lap endless resources for expanding local infrastructure—airports, bullet trains, superhighways, and the like.

Addiction of the magnitude demonstrated by Aomori rarely cures itself by exposure to rational argument. How, then, to get there from here? Going "cold turkey"—that is, suddenly closing the the spigot and keeping it closed—is not a workable proposition. If the goal is to move from a 70 percent or so redistribution of income cross-region to something on the order of Germany's 2 to 3 percent, we are talking about at least a ten-year process of infrastructure deregulation and privatization coupled with a consistent, annual decrease from the national till of 7 percent or so. Enforcing that steadily tightening discipline is a role that the center in Tokyo can usefully play.

And must play. There is no benefit in swinging from the extreme of central control to the extreme of decentralized chaos. There is no virtue in having autonomous regional railroads build networks of track different in gauge from those in adjoining regions, as happened in India and Australia. Or in having regional power grids that vary, one from the next, in current and voltage.

The idea, after all, is to purge the national system, steadily and re-morselessly, of its addiction without creating side effects worse than the original disease. What this means, in practice, is that the center must not only keep tightening the spigot; it must also maintain common standards—in banking, infrastructure, and the like—where they already exist and establish them where they do not. (In Kansai, for example, reflecting U.S. influence, electric current now runs at 60 cycles; in the Tokyo area, reflecting British influence, it runs at 50.) At the same time, in its international dealings, the center must remove the barriers that keep the global economy at bay. Breaking the current addiction is only half the battle. The other half is establishing a healthy, sustainable regime, which cannot be done without inviting that economy in and leveraging its resources.

For Japan, there is no time to lose. All the warning signs are clearly in sight. First, the central control and coordination that make sense up to a GNP per capita level of US $5,000 or so quickly become problematic above it. The interval between that level and OECD status at US $10,000 is very short: Japan did it in less than ten years; Taiwan, Hong Kong, and Singapore in about five. The global system pushes its way in, and there is precious little time to get ready—psychologically, culturally, administratively, organizationally. Although, by a kind of fluke, Japan never really had to make all these adjustments at the time, its own economic problems and pressure from the global economy demand that it do so now.

Second, the balance between wealth generation and wealth distribution is out of kilter: well more than 90 percent of the country receives rather than creates. And third, its economic system is increasingly at odds with global logic. Trade is not open; the value put on land is insupportably high; the price/earnings multiples of corporate equity reflect these inflated—and by now thoroughly unreal—property prices, not the underlying wealth-generating capacity of the businesses themselves; the central government, fearful of a stock market crash, pumps in pension funds and postal savings funds to keep up the price of the Nikkei; and the products and services these businesses deliver to consumers no longer provide the value they seek.

This last warning sign is particularly troubling. The experience of region states, by virtue of their greater openness to the borderless world, reveals with stark clarity the lines along which global flows of economic activity now proceed. No economic system incompatible with them can long continue to prosper. Thus, to the extent that the central governments of nation states still have a key role to play in economic affairs, it is to help break down that incompatibility wherever it exists.

HALF-EATEN CAKE

Defining the center's role in this way implies giving far more economic autonomy to regions. At a minimum, they have to be free to raise capital, build infrastructure, and attract investment. In the United States, for example, there is ample precedent for this. When a city or country decides that it needs an airport, it raises the necessary funds through bonds that it issues and guarantees. In Japan, by contrast, modifying a highway on Hokkaido requires permission that can be granted only in Tokyo.

The middle course that countries like China have found acceptable is to allow greater economic autonomy while keeping the political system unchanged. This has, more or less, worked so far. Certainly, it has worked much better than the awkward, inconsistent movement toward both political and economic liberalization in the former Soviet Union. Even so, it is an inherently unstable compromise. Knowing that you cannot eat your cake and have it too, China has left half of it on the plate. Neither hunger nor aspiration is satisfied.

It is hard to let the global system in only partway. The regions most eager to link up with it will resent all the more any attempt to extract resources from them to be used in funding the civil minimum elsewhere. The eyes of Dalian are on competitors in Singapore and Taiwan, not on propping up loss-making enterprises in Hunan or Hubei. And there will be many more such loss-making enterprises. As both China and the former East Germany have discovered, when you shine the light of world-class competition on enterprise-level socialist accounting, you do see plenty of red—red ink. Being able to take advantage of the global system means making the internal changes necessary to harness its resources and expertise, and these changes, in turn, require a degree of local freedom of action that inevitably collides with a determination to retain firm political control at the center.

The rush to liberalize simultaneously on both sides of the equation, as in the former Soviet Union, can easily become a recipe for chaos. The effort to do things in series, first in the economic sphere and only later in the political, as in China, is a more workable but still ultimately unstable compromise. What, then, should the center do? Is there a sustainable— and tolerable—middle course? If so, it would certainly depend, in the first instance, on removing all discussions of ideology from the table.

This is not an occasion for debating the theoretical merits of communism versus democracy or of state control versus free markets. It is a time for focusing on what works, on what has shown itself best able to improve a people's quality of life. The need at the center is not for theory, but for leadership—in particular, for the articulation both of a country-specific vision of what success would look like 10 or 15 or 20 years from now—Malaysia's "Look East" program, for example—and of a plausible road map for the transition process. In the absence of both road map and vision, no one really knows the direction in which things are supposed to head or the kinds of behavior that are acceptable—or the kinds of obligations that are expected to be met—along the way. And in the absence of such knowledge, order crumbles, gangsterism flourishes, and pressure builds to reassert central control.

In a global economy, the visions of success that work start from a full and open admission of the value of region states and of their need for considerable freedom of action. They also start from a clear appreciation of the kinds of value that only a central government can appropriately provide—military security, for instance, a sound currency, infrastructure standards, and the like.

This admission and appreciation lead inexorably to one or another form of federation as the only type of "umbrella" political organization under which multiple region states can independently flourish in the context of a global economy and yet still be linked with the broader national interest. With no such umbrella in place, either the progress of individual region states will be retarded (which, of course, defeats the whole purpose of the exercise) or the behaviors triggered by their separate achievement of each new rung of the GNP per capita ladder will allow precious resources to flow to moneymaking opportunities elsewhere in the world. If Shanghai's concern is only for the good fortune of Shanghai-based investors, there may be opportunities in, say, Vietnam, that offer unbeatably attractive returns on their investment of money and skill.

If a strong federal center exists, however, it can guide this transition process and, in an orderly fashion, relax either the degree or the nature of its control as each new GNP plateau is reached and the externally imposed discipline of global logic takes hold. The temptation for the center, certainly, will be to hold on too long and to substitute its own priorities or preferences for that discipline. Both responses are predictable, and both have predictable results: they will scare the global economy away. It may be a new feeling for those at the center, but the proper response to a federated region's closer—and GNP level-calibrated—integration with the global economy ought be: Wonderful, another problem we don't have to worry about. In that way— and only in that way—will there be cake enough for everyone.

THE "HOLLOWING OUT" OF SERVICES

In the past year or so, freeing up regions, under a federal umbrella, to achieve a suitable division of baked goods has taken on a sudden new urgency. Several decades before, when Japan and the Four Tigers first began to assert their competitiveness in the manufacturing sector, the industrialized nation states began to worry that many of their domestic manufacturing industries would begin to "hollow out"—that is, to migrate, piece of business system by piece of business system—to lower-wage or higher-skill environments offshore.

At home, the first thing to go would be the traditional blue-collar jobs in production and assembly that had long been the mainstay of these countries' economies. Sooner or later, however, engineering would follow manufacturing only to be followed, in turn, by R&D. The initial slow, if noisy, leak would steadily grow larger and louder until it reached the intolerable level of the "giant sucking sound" that, according to Ross Perot, would characterize the southward plunge of manufacturing jobs from the United States if NAFTA were approved.

Fears over this hollowing out process could be offset, to some extent, by the recognition that such migrations were, after all, a natural part of an industry's life cycle in a given national environment. If the economy were resilient in the face of such pressures, two things would happen. First, there would be a general revitalization of the manufacturing sector that would restore—or, perhaps, improve—value-added competitiveness, even if it did not replace all the low-end jobs that had been lost. And second, the economy as a whole would migrate toward ever-greater reliance—both for new jobs and for future growth—on the knowledge-intensive service sector.

After all, these nations had had many years in which to enjoy the benefits of their vibrant industrial sectors. Moreover, as they migrated up the ladder of development, a steadily larger share of GNP and employment would inevitably come from services. This was a perfectly natural process of transformation. Heightened competition merely hastened it along.

Even so, addicted as they are to the civil minimum and politically vulnerable to calls for subsidy and protection, the governments of nation states have had great difficulty with this sort of transformation. It doesn't come cheap, and it doesn't come without a great deal of pain. But it is unavoidable. And, at the end of the road, is a high value-added, knowledge-intensive, 21st-century service economy. So the game *is* worth the candle.

But what if, along the way, after only a few years of development, even these service industries began to hollow out—that is, what if the constraints of developing them under the umbrella of traditional nation states began to drive them to more hospitable environments? This would not be a natural part of the transformation process. It would come much too soon. It would short-circuit the cycle of growth. And it would raise fundamental questions about the long-term viability of these states as political, as well as economic, units. These questions now have to be asked because the hollowing out of services has already begun.

Some of this migration of service activities is the result of the lifestyle choices made by the highly skilled knowledge workers most critical to them. In the United States, for example, the migration of software development to Santa Clara, Colorado, and the Pacific Northwest is the result of the fact that leading-edge companies have set up programming shops there, and these areas make a convenient gateway to Asia-Pacific, much as Glasgow has become a gateway to single-market Europe. But it also derives from the obvious preference of world-class professionals for the kind of outdoor lifestyle that such regions offer. In fact, a recent *Business Week* survey found that, among American executives, the city of Seattle is now the favored location in which to live and work.

But this migration is also being driven by powerful economic and technological forces—especially so in those industries that are most inherently borderless. Nearly a third of the major Italian corporations that issue equity for public sale do so in London, not in Italy. The market—and the mechanics—at home are not sufficiently attractive. Similarly, in 1993 and 1994, more than 20 percent of the transactions involving companies listed on the Tokyo Stock Exchange took place in London (and another little bit in Hong Kong and Singapore), and more than 90 percent of new Japanese corporate bonds were issued in Europe.

Using modern technology, companies based in Italy or Japan can access various London or New York markets with increasingly transparent ease. Why shouldn't they? After all, U.S. firms have for years had ready access not just to the NYSE, but also to various regional exchanges, futures markets, commodities markets in Chicago, NAS-

DAQ, the American Stock exchange, the Eurodollar markets, and the offshore financial services provided by Bermuda, the Cayman Islands, and the Bahamas.

Traditional nation states are extremely porous to migrations of this sort. The footprints of satellite-based TV broadcasting do not respect political borders. Nor do the logistics of computer diagnosis and maintenance, which can now be provided from remote locations through the Internet and charged against Visa and MasterCard. Nor does the telecom network capacity made available by global telecom players. For consumers living even in still-protected markets like Japan, several companies based in Colorado are already offering low-est-cost routing (LCR) services for international phone calls at something like half the established rate. Nor do the wishes of Japanese consumers to avoid the cartel-like pricing structure that so inflates the cost of their international airline tickets. (Today, more than half the international tickets used by Japanese citizens are bought either overseas or through the network in dollars. The government does, however, have rules against buying, say, a Seoul to Los Angeles ticket, with a stop in Tokyo—because it is much cheaper than a Tokyo/Los Angeles ticket—and then never using the Seoul portion.) Nor do the banking needs of Japanese consumers, who find even the ATMs of their domestic banks closed between 7 p.m. and 8 a.m., as well as over the weekend—in other words, just when they need them most. With 1-800 access, however, they can now use the automated systems of American banks at any hour of the day for the majority of their non-cash-in-hand transactions.

Nor, for that matter, do the distribution systems for many consumer products. People anywhere can now select items from printed catalogs, CD-ROM disks, or on-line listings, order them through phone or fax or computer, and make payment through the international settlement function of major credit cards. In fact, my reform movement in Japan, the Reform of Heisei,[3] has established a members'club—the TONBO Club—for just this purpose. *Tonbo* in Japanese means dragonfly. But its initials also stand for Technology Obsoletes National Borders.

This is a self-reinforcing process. Given these possibilities, demand for locally generated services will inevitably hollow out. But in a bor-derless economy, supply—the provision of these services—will hollow out as well. It will, sooner or later, move away from geographical areas that impose undue restraint. Unless there is dramatic change in the policies of Japan's Ministry of Transportation, for example, this is exactly what will happen to the country's airline industry. At the moment, virtually everything is still tightly regulated: the number of Japan-based international airlines permitted to operate, the pairs of cities between which service is permitted, the airports (there are now 15 of them) from which international flights are permitted to particular destinations, passenger loads, flight schedules, and even what kind of food can be served on the plane to different classes of passengers.

In economic terms, this is inefficient, costly, and uncompetitive nonsense: Japan's national carriers have a cost base, per passenger mile, twice that of their leading competitors. Not surprisingly, their share of the global market is falling, and they are simply unable to provide the range of services from the range of airports that their customers want. In practice, even with yen-denominted ticket prices 40 to 50 percent higher than their dollar-denominated equivalents, they cannot take advantage of the great opportunities for growth so abundantly available in the booming Asia-Pacific region. Indeed, virtually all of the recently added services between different regions in Japan and a host of new destinations in Asia are being provided by Asiana Airlines, Singapore Airlines, Dragonair, China Airlines, and so on. JAL and ANA just limp along.

Worse, to ease the pain caused by so noticeable a limp, the government has chosen to subsidize JAL and ANA's losses in international operations by allowing them to keep domestic ticket prices ludicrously high. It now costs more to make a round trip between Tokyo and Okinawa than between Tokyo and Los Angeles or Chicago. Moreover, for an Osaka resident, a vacation in Guam or Saipan—hotel and airfare included—is less than half the cost of a comparable stay on Okinawa. This means, of course, that fewer tourists will go to Okinawa, the island's economy will suffer, and the central government will have to pour in yet more money to fund the civil minimum. It is cheaper for a Tokyo family to go to Whistler, British Columbia, to ski than to go to Hokkaido, if the stay is longer than five days. This is worse than nonsense; it is idiocy. Everybody loses: citizens, consumers, travelers, entrepreneurs, investors, taxpayers, potential entrants, and the established airlines themselves. True, the fig leaf of central control remains in place. But all it is covering is an airline sector that is rapidly hollowing out.

How much more sensible it would be to relax that control. If the Kansai area around Osaka wanted to buy—or start up—its own airline to facilitate region-based international travel, why not let it? Kansai's economy, after all, is larger than that of Canada, and Canada has two airlines of its own. Or why not allow Kansai to buy into—or initiate a joint venture with—a major international carrier like British Airways or United Airlines and run its Asian operations out of the regional hub in Osaka? Everyone would be better served. It would be to everyone's advantage—except, of course, the bureaucrats.

Much the same is true in financial services. Legally, a Japanese national cannot have an overseas bank account, unless he or she is temporarily living abroad. That is what the rule says—a rule made decades ago, long before the Japanese financial markets were liberalized. Why, then, is it that the Ministry of Finance keeps this old rule? To maintain control, of course.

Even so, the vast majority of credit card transactions are processed by American companies. So are most other cross-border transactions. Product-by-product regulation, which is the norm in Japan, makes little sense in a world where money can instantaneously transform itself, chameleon-like, into countless different forms. It will only drive those services away. It has been doing just that. Meanwhile, we could have an active Asian bond market on Kyushu. And regional development bonds, like those issued by Kansai, could be made far more attractive if they weren't bought primarily by the postal savings system. A standing arrangement whereby one part of the government buys another part of the government's paper is fundamentally uninteresting to outside investors. They will take their money and their business elsewhere.

Consider still another example: the government-owned and -managed postal service in Japan. It, too, is an uncompetitive relic. Left unchanged, the services it provides will inevitably hollow out. As of April 1994, the domestic surface rate went up from 62 yen to 80 yen—that is, roughly 80 cents per first-class letter, compared to 32 cents in the United States, a country many times its physical size. To calibrate, remember that airmail from the United States to Japan is 95 cents and from Hong Kong to Tokyo, 50 cents.

Thus, for a direct marketer in Japan, it is significantly cheaper to airmail in bulk from the United States than from the next block in Tokyo. This goes beyond even idiocy; this is insanity. If it happens, the printing, layout, and design work will quickly follow—if they have not already done so. True to its heritage, the government has responded to this threat of a postal-based hollowing out of services not by fixing the problems with the country's mail system, but by passing a law to make illegal the bulk mailing of direct-marketing materials into Japan by Japanese firms. It thinks the solution is arrest. I think its solution is arrested development. But in the Internet society, the passage of such a law is to no avail. Direct mail can be "file transferred" to Hong Kong or the United States electronically and then individually mailed to Japanese consumers. Hence, the new law is virtually meaningless.

For the past decade or two, U.S. managers and policymakers alike have been visibly and vocally worried about the hollowing out of the nation's manufacturing sector. On all sides, the fear has been that work that used to be done in domestic plants and factories would migrate to lower-wage locations in Latin America or Asia-Pacific. About a comparable hollowing out of the service sector, however, there has been virtually no sign—due, in large part, to the unparalleled competitive strength of many U.S. service-based industries. For Europe, Japan, and even the Asian tigers, however, the situation is altogether different. Unless their governments move quickly to deregulate key service sectors so that sheltered domestic players can grow strong from more intense competition, these activities—by far the largest segment of their economies—will migrate cross-border in a very short period of time.

In the 19th century, the primary form of cross-border economic migration was the movement of huge numbers of people across the ocean from one country to another. In the late 20th century, it has been the movement of corporations in search of low-cost production sites. In the early 21st century, by contrast, it will be the movement of knowledge-intensive services through global digital networks. Unlike the movement of people and even of production, both or which are slow processes measured in years and perhaps decades, the transmigration of these services can literally happen overnight.

This is a sobering fact for central governments to deal with. It cannot help but discipline them. After all, in Japan, nearly 65 percent of the working population is engaged in the service sector, and many of the jobs officially listed as belonging to the manufacturing sector—engineering and marketing, for example—are really service jobs. Because all this work is vulnerable to extremely fast cross-border migration on the digital network, the governments of 19th-century-style nation states must increasingly hear the powerful and insistent voice of global logic. The open question, of course, is whether they have lost the ability to listen.

FROM PRIME MOVER TO CATALYST

So long as nation states continue to view themselves as the essential prime movers in economic affairs, so long as they resist—in the name of national interest—any erosion of central control as a threat to sovereignty, neither they nor their people will be able to harness the full resources of the global economy. This is not the road to prosperity and an improved quality of life. It is an admission that the cancer of protection, subsidy, and the civil minimum has grown so large and spread so widely that it has become inoperable. There is, of course, another, much happier choice: to embrace the global economy, to react with pleasure to the development of local ports of entry to that economy, and to do everything possible to encourage and nurture the successful operation of those ports—those region states. In other words, there is, indeed, a healthy and vital role for nation states: to be an effective catalyst for the activities of regions.

In the United States, aggressive moves to deregulate the economy and a long history of state-level decentralization under a federal umbrella are excellent preparation for this kind of catalyst role. Forty-seven of its 50 states, for example, now have their own representatives in Japan. Even so, the voices coming out of Washington, influenced as they are by politically influential pleas for help from depressed regions and distressed industries, still tend to sing a different tune. The song is extremely costly: each job saved through government action in the domestic automobile industry has cost taxpayers roughly $80,000. Worse, if it continues, this protectionist chorus will drive even leading-edge, knowledge-intensive companies in service industries to the more favorable environment of countries like Malaysia and Singapore.

This continued "official" influence of this chorus is particularly frustrating, given the great strides the U.S. economy has made at the unofficial, grassroots level to adapt itself to the new global realities. Thirty million Americans now work from their homes, many for lifestyle and even tax reasons, and are linked to customers and employers by phone and fax and modem. Among them are thousands upon thousands of managers and technologists who left the payrolls of large, established companies as they went through ambitious downsizing programs during the past decade or so. These newly independent professionals have brought to their current areas of activity both capital and an unprecedented level of expertise. They are not flipping hamburgers for low wages; they are building tomorrow's network-based businesses—and creating many new jobs in the process.

The temptation, of course, is to run to Washington for help. For certain kinds of issues—foreign trade restrictions, hurricane damage in Florida, geological and social earthquakes in Los Angeles—this makes perfect sense. Most of the time, however, it does not. Whatever real "solutions" exist can be found in the global economy through ports of entry at the regional level. Is the Massachusetts economy suffering from defense cutbacks? Why not work to make New England a "window" for European investment in America, in the same way that Glasgow provides a window for resources flowing the other way? Is farm income hurting in Arkansas or Louisiana? Why not band together with the same type of humid growing areas in adjacent states, invite in Japanese capital, and initiate a rice-crop joint venture with Japanese growers? If states and localities compete against each other for investment, as they usually do, outsiders can always play off both ends against the middle. But if they act on behalf of their shared regional interests—and regions, remember, are the right level of aggregation for tapping global logic and for generating economies of service—everyone benefits.

In Canada, the contentious debate over the status of Quebec has made it difficult to think—let alone talk—about regional issues in a constructive way. Yet the clear message of the most recent elections is that national policy is disaggregating along strongly regional lines. Cracks and fissures are already beginning to show along the country's horizontal lines of stress. The thin band of the country within, say, 100 miles of the U.S. border, now looks south to NAFTA. Quebec, of course, looks east to France. Ontario is effectively part of the American Midwest. And the Far West looks to Asia-Pacific. Not surprisingly, in British Columbia, large numbers of parents want the schools to teach their children Chinese, Japanese, and Korean. But the national constitution demands that they all be taught French and English. What, then, holds Canada together as a country? If it has no mission to catalyze these regional economies, what mission does it have?

Australia is another delicate situation. True, it has a long history of regional—that is, federal state-based—autonomy, but the dividing lines between these geographical units have little to do with achieving better access to the four I's. There is, for example, a genuine rivalry between Sydney and Melbourne—over the selection of host city for the Olympic Games, for example. But it is a parochial, inward-looking rivalry. What the two should be thinking about, instead, is the other regions in Asia-Pacific with which each should be forging close economic linkages. New Zealand, long characterized by protectionist policies, has at last woken up to the global economy and learned a great deal, not from Australia or the United Kingdom, but from Singapore. Its population of 3.4 million is a good size for the country to operate effectively as a region state in a global economy.

In Europe, for nearly four decades, the continent's leaders have been trying to implement the Treaty of Rome. But they have been outrun by events. By the time they made significant headway in linking up 12 national economies, the global migration of the four I's had made national, as opposed to regional, economies far less relevant to movement up the ladder of development. Thus, just when nation states began to lose their primacy as economic actors, Brussels created a supernation state. This is ironic. It is also tragic. Of all the developed world, Europe has the richest and densest history of regionalism. Europe, after all, is where regional interests first combined to create the modern nation state. In a borderless world, it could draw upon and leverage that heritage with immense profit. Instead, it has purposely organized itself to stamp that heritage out.

Even before enlargement, the area defined by the shared interests of the EU's 12 central governments is narrow enough. But when that small patch is reduced further to reflect just the areas of overlap among regional interests, what's left as the basis for a common European economic policy is a miniscule lowest common denominator indeed. It is silly to presume that the same policies will bring prosperity to all parts of Spain or Italy. Demonstrably, they do not—and cannot. What they will do, however, is lock into place a cascading series of governmental levels, all of which are inextricably committed to providing the civil minimum to various sets of claimants.

Asia, by contrast, is the part of the world where current levels of prosperity are most obviously region-based. In Indonesia, per capita GNP varies by as much as a factor of six between regions; in China, by as much as a factor of 20. That is why Asian leaders are proving so responsive to the establishment of cross-border economic zones. They know they cannot hope to drive every part of their countries in lock-step—and at a constant speed—into the global economy. But they can support and encourage a host of separate, region-based initiatives to join the global economy, at least sequentially.

In practice, this has meant accepting the fact that the overwhelmingly center-driven model represented by postwar Japan is no longer relevant to the experience of Asia's newly emerging economies. The limits of Japan's approach are clearer now; the four I's are much further developed; cultural and ethnic linkages play a more important "enabling" role; and local needs are much more visible to—and much more able to attract—support from the global economy. Central government, as well as central government-mediated access to multilateral agencies, is no longer the only game in town. As a result, there is no longer a single head bird in the flock of Asian "flying geese."

China, of course, is the massive question mark. Is the current warmth of its economy the mark of a late spring or of an Indian summer just before the frost? At the moment, regional initiatives flourish, but the government has not yet proven that it has learned its lesson about intervening with a heavy hand—or about how disruptive it is to change course every so often on tax policy or other forms of regula-

140 The End of the Nation State

tion. Nor, for that matter, have outside investors learned not to overestimate the true extent to which things have been liberalized. The signs are inconsistent.

They are inconsistent, too, in Taiwan, which should really be operating as two or three powerful separate region states, e.g., Taipei, Taichung, and Kaohsiung under the umbrella of a Chinese commonwealth. And in India, where there has been a less explicit commitment than in China to region-based development and where both the political and the macroeconomic environment are not entirely stable. And in Brazil, where the central government's refusal to move toward a commonwealth form of organization is holding São Paulo back from joining the OECD and so helping to bring prosperity to the rest of the country.

There is still time for central governments to embrace their new role as regional catalysts, but it is growing short. In South Korea, for example, with its strong centralist tradition, the new law on regional autonomy that came into effect on January 1, 1995, did not go far enough. Individual regions are still not free to make their own arrangements with the global economy.

At the moment, this represents only an opportunity lost. But when, sooner or later, South Korea has to deal with economic integration with the north, it will have the choice of following the German route and absorbing all costs itself or of inviting in the global economy and so sharing the burden. The sheer magnitude of the burden implied by following the German route is sobering. But that burden cannot be avoided if everything is left to the last minute. The global economy will want to see a coherent, region-based plan solidly in place before it jumps in with support. Wait too long, as Germany did, and global logic will find desperate, after-the-fact, jury-rigged cases for support thoroughly unconvincing.

In today's borderless world, the lesson for central governments is clear: hold onto economic control too long, and it becomes worthless. Burdens increase, and no one will pay for them but you. Give it up early, however, or better, transmute it into one or another form of catalysis, and the global economy will rush in to help.

Epilogue

A SWING OF THE PENDULUM

In the broad sweep of history, nation states have been a transitional form of organization for managing economic affairs. Their right—their prerogative—to manage them grew, in part, out of the control of military strength, but such strength is now an uncomfortably great burden to maintain. (It has also largely been exposed as a means to preserve the positions of those in power, not to advance the quality-of-life interests of their people.) Their right grew out of the control of natural resources and colonies, but the first is relatively unimportant as a source of value in a knowledge-intensive economy, and the second is less a source of low-cost resources than a bottomless drain on the home government's treasury. It grew out of the control of land, but prosperous economies can spread their influence through neighboring territories without any need for adjustment in formal divisions of sovereignty. And it grew out of the control of political independence, but such independence is of diminishing importance in a global economy that has less and less respect for national borders.

Moreover, as it grew, the nation state's organizational right to manage economic affairs fell victim to an inescapable cycle of decay. This should occasion no surprise. It comes as close to being a natural law as the messy universe of political economy allows. Whatever the form of government in power and whatever the political ideology that

141

shapes it, demands for the civil minimum, for the support of special interests, and for the subsidization and protection of those left behind inexorably rise. In different circumstances, under different regimes, and during different eras, the speed of escalation varies. Good policy can slow the pace, bad policy can accelerate it. But no policy can stop it altogether. Nation states are political organisms, and in their economic bloodstreams cholesterol steadily builds up. Over time, arteries harden and the organism's vitality decays.

History, of course, also records the kinds of catastrophic, equilibrium-busting events that can stop or even reverse this aging process. Wars can do it, as can natural disasters like plagues, earthquakes, and volcanic eruptions. They have certainly done so in the past. But even for the most cold-blooded practitioners of *realpolitik,* these are hardly credible as purposeful instruments of economic policy.

Thus, in today's borderless economy, with its rapid cross-border migration of the four I's, there is really only one strategic degree of freedom that central governments have to counteract this remorseless buildup of economic cholesterol, only one legitimate instrument of policy to restore sustainable and self-reinforcing vitality, only one practical as well as morally acceptable way to meet their people's near-term needs without mortgaging the long-term prospects of their children and grandchildren. And that is to cede meaningful operational autonomy to the wealth-generating region states that lie within or across their borders, to catalyze the efforts of those region states to seek out global solutions, and to harness their distinctive ability to put global logic first and to function as ports of entry to the global economy. The only hope is to reverse the postfeudal, centralizing tendencies of the modern era and allow—or better, encourage—the economic pendulum to swing away from nations and back toward regions.

THE COMING TEST

Many will find this swing of the pendulum uncomfortable and unwelcome. It challenges the established networks of power and influence within nation states. It challenges the established questions about which the citizens of those states are asked to vote. It challenges the usual way in which the leaders of those states try to manage cross-bor-

EXHIBIT E–1

Optimal Operating Unit Changes as We Move from the Industrial to the Information Age

	Old Game	Rise of the Region-State*	New Game
	Industrial Age		**Information Age**
Timing	19–20th century		Late 20th–21st century
Description	• Driven by nation-state governments		• Driven by private capital and information
	• National sovereignty		• Citizen sovereignty
	• Strong control by centralized forces		• Autonomous networks of interdependent private enterprises and regional entities
	• Sensitive to borders		• Inherently borderless
	• Favors domestic capital and protects domestic companies		• Welcomes foreign capital and world-class companies/expertise, creating high-quality jobs
	• Aims for one-state prosperity through development of export-led, manufacturing-driven economic growth		• Aims for harmonious regional prosperity based on interdependent, network-centric companies creating information-intensive services to capture value from customers
	• Government initiatives		• Entrepreneurial initiatives
	• Good government strengthens priority industries		• Good government nurtures regional development, not focused in specific industry
	• Change occurs gradually over decades		• Change occurs suddenly in months to years
Winners	• Germany		• Hong Kong/Shenzhen
	• Japan/"New Japans"		• Singapore/Johor/Batam
	• United Kingdom		• Taiwan/Fujian
	• United States		• Southern China (Pearl River Delta)
			• Southern India (e.g., Bangalore)
			• North Mexico/Southwestern U.S.
			• Silicon Valley
			• New Zealand
			• Lombardia
			• Pacific Northwest of the United States

*Region-state is defined as an area (often cross-border) developed around a regional economic center with a population of a few million to 10–20 million.

der flows of activity, as well as the currency exchange rates associated with those flows. And it challenges the fundamental rationale of the multilateral institutions in which nation states participate—the U.N., for example, and the OECD, and new groupings like the EU, NAFTA, and APEC.

In fact, even where there are relatively few vested interests to threaten, as with those constituencies dispassionately worried about the most economically backward areas of the world—the abject poverty, overpopulation, and thoughtless pollution of sub-Saharan Africa, for example—it challenges the established tool kit of remedial policies. But here, too, country-focused solutions have amply demonstrated their inadequacies. As the philosopher William James might have said, wealth, like knowledge, grows in spots and spreads out from there. Today, in the developing as in the developed world, the natural business unit for tapping the global economy to produce wealth is the region, not the nation.

Much rides on how well these challenges are met. After Hong Kong reverts to China in 1997, for example, policies that respect and try to leverage global logic will help spread its recipe for economic success to the rest of the country. But policies that ignore that logic in favor of efforts to maintain heavy-handed control by the central government will, just as easily, crush Hong Kong's prosperity and, in so doing, deprive the rest of China of its best example—and most powerful locomotive—of economic progress. It is by no means clear that Beijing has gotten the message. In the present, politically unstable environment, the overwhelming temptation for those at the center is to defend aggressively every last bit of political sovereignty, and thus to treat Hong Kong very much as an "internal" problem and not as an opportunity to harness outward-looking global logic.

No matter how politically appealing, however, such inward- or nation state-focused solutions are, in economic terms, simply not sustainable. As the economist Paul Krugman has recently argued, for example, the great Asian success stories of the past few decades—Singapore, Hong Kong, and so on—were largely the result of massive, one-off, and unrepeatable improvements in factor inputs. Much like the forgotten success stories of Eastern Europe during the 1950s, huge levels of investment, made possible by high savings rates, fundamentally changed the productivity of labor. At the same time, huge numbers of people were brought into the work force who had never been in the work force before, and huge increases in educational levels boosted the economic value these new workers could create.

By definition, these massive changes in inputs do not represent policy choices that can be implemented over and over again. Hence, according to Krugman, the Asian "miracle," though impressive, cannot be sustained. Now, Krugman's facts are exactly right—but they are facts about the economies of nation states, not region states. If you average these one-off changes in factor inputs across the whole of a national economy, they are not repeatable. But if you localize them to the relevant regions within or across that nation's borders, there will be many other regions in which ample progress still can be made.

Equally important, Krugman's argument assumes that such progress is to be measured against only one generic model of Asia-Pacific economic development: Japan. But the idea that the whole region is, in effect, like a flock of flying geese, all trailing along on the same course at one or another distance behind the head goose of Japan, is badly out of date. There are now many different head geese, each leading the way along a unique and distinctive course. And each of these geese has, over the years, changed its course many times—in Singapore's case, for example, from labor value-added to service value-added, and then to information value-added. Thus, to argue that past improvements must, of necessity, run out of steam is to ignore these variations between and within different models of development.

HOW ARTERIES HARDEN

On a recent flight from Tokyo to Portland, Oregon, I sat next to a young attorney from Livingston, Montana, a small city that was the site of Robert Redford's fly-fishing movie, "A River Runs Through It." She was on her way back home after visiting Livingston's sister city, Naganohara, in Gunma Prefecture. The differences between these two cities, as she summed them up, were quite instructive. Both had populations of about 7,000 and collected about the same amount of annual tax revenue. Livingston, however, had a yearly budget of US $2 million, no full-time representatives, and a part-time mayor (who was also a sawmill worker). By contrast, Naganohara had a budget of US $38.7 million, 18 full-time representatives, and a full-time mayor with an annual salary of more than US $125,000. Much the same is true of all the 3,300 towns and municipalities in Japan: the apparatus of local administration, which is wildly out of proportion to the municipal tax base, is made possible only by funds distributed from Tokyo—in exchange, of course, for strict local adherence to the policies and procedures of the central government.

And what do each of Japan's 3,300 towns and cities do with this money? First, whether they need them or not, they build bridges and roads and schools and public auditoriums. But why stop there? Whatever their climate, they build indoor baseball fields, libraries, museums, and concert halls. But there is still more to spend. So they build dams and irrigation facilities, slap ugly concrete structures on all available hillsides to prevent theoretically possible avalanches, and slap even uglier concrete barriers along the banks of streams and rivers to prevent theoretically possible floods. As a result, little sand or gravel washes down to the sea to replace the eroding shoreline (the country loses 1 percent of its natural shoreline each year). This means, of course, still more money has to be spent slapping still uglier structures—tetrapods that look like immense concrete grenades—all along the coastline. More than half of Japan's coastline today is manmade.

Taken together, this orgy of construction, most of it unnecessary and little of it devoted to producing the affordable housing that our citizens do need, eats up some US $850 billion a year—roughly half of the country's national budget. When Japan was recovering from the war, construction activity of this magnitude made plausible economic sense. Today, it does not. It does, however, make perfect political sense: the entrenched Japanese political system is highly dependent on the votes of—and, far more important, on monetary contributions from—the nation's 530,000 construction companies. In all of this, the people's interest in a better quality of life is both unaddressed and invisible. The "bureau-tatorship" in Tokyo, however, is extremely well served. To them, even the harsh demands of U.S. trade negotiators that Japan significantly boost its domestic consumption sound like a narcotic fantasy. The LDP and the bureau-tators would like nothing better than to use the United States as yet another excuse to sprinkle still more concrete structures throughout the country.

At the same time, remember, the yen/dollar exchange rate is in the neighborhood of 95, rather than 180 or so—the level justified by the yen's purchasing power parity, according to both the World Bank and the OECD. This difference of nearly a factor of two is a pretty good measure of the success of the government's explicit policy to place the interests of its citizen/consumers second to the those of its favored industries, which are expected to drive the country's wealth creation. At a much earlier stage of economic development, this may have been legitimate policy. But today, at US $30,000 GNP per capita, it is not.

A construction-focused political system, together with the legal and regulatory mechanisms that enable crazed levels of land speculation, puts the interests of Japan's bureau-tators, not its citizens, first. An economic policy that favors industries over consumers does the same. Together, they send the same message: if the established powers that be prosper, the country prospers and, ultimately, so do its citizens. By now, however, the jury is in and the verdict is clear: it does not, and they do not. Land is not affordable, housing is not available, and the real, daily quality of life lags well behind where it should be given the country's overall economic performance.

In a word, Japan's economic arteries have hardened, and its gridlock of vested interests is nearly impossible to untangle from the center. As a practical matter, the country's Fair Trade Commission cannot begin to touch the cartel in cement or the oligopoly among suppliers of construction materials or aluminum window sashes or bathroom fixtures or sheet glass. How could it, when the arteries are almost completely clogged? In 1992, for example, when the general contractor and Sagawa scandals shook the LDP, the heads of all the major economic forums in Tokyo represented regulated and protected industries: the head of the Keidanren was the chairman of Tokyo Electric Company, the largest utility monopoly in the world; the head of the Chamber of Commerce was the chairman of Japan's largest general contractor; and the head of the Nikkeiren was the chairman of Japan's leading cement company. Moreover, two of the three top members of the Doyukai came from the Bank of Japan and a cement company.

This is, perhaps, an extreme case, but it illustrates a general point:

even political systems that begin by trying to serve the economic interests of all of their citizens become paralyzed over time by the buildup of cholesterol represented by special interests, subsidy, protection, and the civil minimum. This buildup can take many different forms—the social programs of the Scandinavian economies, the "social contract" of German labor unions, the cartel-ridden economy of Switzerland[1], the farm lobby in France, the construction industry and the rice farmers in Japan, or the defense industry in the United States. Whatever its form, once it has progressed beyond a certain limited threshold, it becomes well-nigh impossible to reverse.

So long as they limit themselves to the normal policy tools and processes, the governments of nation states are powerless to break up the masses clogging their economic arteries. They can, however, look to region states to do the job for them. Much as corporations, which are also vulnerable to such unhealthy buildups, can shake themselves up from time to time by reorganizing in a different fashion—from functional organization to divisionalization, from country-based to worldwide product groups—countries can also shake themselves up by choosing to follow a new kind of organizational logic—that is, by redefining their role from that of central provider to that of region state catalyst.

Does such a change—such a swing of the pendulum—solve all problems? Of course not. But it does free up energies that would otherwise be unavailable. Will the new regime, in time, create problems of its own? Of course it will. But these can be attacked by further organizational shakeups down the road. And that is exactly the point: these are, at bottom, organizational problems driven by human nature, and they can be solved, or at least ameliorated, by organizational solutions that take human nature into account. They are *not* fundamental questions of ideology that can be resolved only by imposing an ideological answer—liberal democracy, socialist/market economy, communism, or whatever—on the territories of sovereign nation states. The goal, after all, is not to legitimize this or that political establishment or power arrangement. It is to improve the quality of life of people, regular people—us, no matter where they live. People came first; borders came afterwards. It is time for economic policy to remember this simple fact.

Just as the current paralysis of nation states now shows them to have been a transitional mode of organization for managing economic affairs, region states may well outlive their usefulness some time in the future. Nothing is forever. At the moment, however, they are just what the doctor ordered. Given suitable autonomy, region states—by virtue of their unique ability to put global logic first—can provide precisely the kind of change agent the times require: effective engines of prosperity and improved quality of life for the people of the global economy.

Appendix A

WHAT MOVES EXCHANGE RATES?

New Dynamics Challenge Traditional Theories

by Kenichi Ohmae

Since Japan liberalized its foreign exchange (FX) laws in 1980, the yen has joined the Western basket of currency trading. What this means is that about two-thirds of the world's economy is now rather freely interlinked through currency trading. Traditional economic policies based on a closed-country model, such as those of the Keynesians and the monetarists, are being seriously challenged. For example, the existing models cannot explain simple and now not-so-uncommon phenomena, such as these:

- Employment is created in South Korea when the American economy picks up.
- Money appears in the United States overnight when the Japanese money supply is too great.
- The economy recovers while unemployment goes up, due to robots taking over human jobs.
- Currency rates fluctuate more than 40 percent a year when the fundamentals of the two economies — Japan and the U.S. — really haven't changed much.

Reprinted in facsimile from the *Japan Times*, July 29, 1987 (revised December 1989). Used with permission.

I have made some attempts to develop a model to explain the globally interlinked economy. At this stage, I think I have an interesting model for the currency portion of the interlinked economy, which merits critical appraisal from scholars and students of currency trading. Let me describe my basic understanding of the current situation, the assumption in constructing our model, and the results of our initial testing.

The FX Market Begins to Have Its Own Raison d'Etre

A survey conducted by central banks at the end of March 1986 indicates that the trading volume of FX in the three key markets of London, New York and Tokyo was in the order of $200 billion a day. London was the largest of the three at $90 billion, followed by N.Y. at $50 billion to $58 billion and Tokyo at $48 billion to $50 billion.

Foreign exchange trading, along with futures and options, was designed to assist in smoothing international transactions such as trade and investment. Such activities amount, at the most, to only about $20 billion daily among the U.S., Europe and Japan. It cannot possibly explain the current size of the FX market, which is 10 times larger than the volume of real transactions. What has happened is that the FX market has started to have its own *raison d'etre,* and has developed unique behavioral patterns that must be treated with care and interpreted with a new perspective. For example, the FX market has been proven to:

• *Dwarf government intervention.* Against the declining dollar, the Bank of Japan (BOJ) injected some $16 billion to arrest the dollar's free fall from March 19, 1986, through Jan. 29, 1987. During the two-and-a-half weeks at the beginning of 1987, the BOJ injected as much as $8.5 billion to support the dollar, to no avail. The FX market has become an empire of its own, or the Third Empire, which seems completely independent of the Group of Five or, for that matter, any government.

• *Not reflect purchasing power.* As Figure 1 indicates, there is no major item which can justify the current exchange rate of ¥140 to the dollar. In fact, a more reasonable conversion rate is certainly above ¥180, in order to equalize the prices of day-to-day commodities.

There are several reasons for this seemingly perplexing issue. One, and the most obvious, is that the Japanese distribution system is much more extended and less efficient than that of the U.S. Thus, a Japanese-made camera can be purchased at a much

Figure 1 Purchasing Power
¥/$; 1988

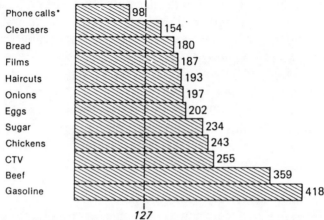

Phone calls*	98
Cleansers	154
Bread	180
Films	187
Haircuts	193
Onions	197
Eggs	202
Sugar	234
Chickens	243
CTV	255
Beef	359
Gasoline	418

127

* Local calls only
Source: *Consumer Price Report '88; Economic Statistics Yearbook;* McKinsey analysis

lower price at the 47th Street Photo Shop in New York City than at Yodobashi Camera, a Tokyo discount store. A typical camera or color TV is priced at four times its manufacturing cost. So, purchasing power, which was believed to influence the currency exchange rate in equalizing prices, needs to be redefined using a product's cost to the importing decision-maker.

International trade occurs based on the competitiveness of a product's delivered cost (i.e., manufacturing plus logistics cost), as opposed to sales price. In order for Japan to increase imports, as the dollar and other currencies gain relative advantage, distribution must be streamlined. The so-called price elasticity due to change in the exchange rate does not occur if the lower or higher price is not passed on to the real purchasing decision-maker. For example, if the delivered price of an American manufacturer's scientific instruments is lowered as a result of a weaker dollar, it may gain a share of the market from its Japanese competitors, and the American export may climb, showing clear signs of elasticity. Likewise, if cotton oil became more competitive than sesame seeds and/or coconut oil, the U.S.-made cotton oil might displace other types of oil as sources, e.g., for making salad oil. So, while the end-user price may not go down, as the middleman pockets the additional profit, elasticity is observed as the exchange rate changes. However, in most cases, a simple reduction in the import price at the cost-insurance-and-freight (CIF) or free-on-board (FOB) levels does not result in increased imports, as little is passed on to the consumers. Indeed, consumers of both West Germany and Japan have not really benefited from the decrease in import prices as their currencies have strengthened, as shown in Figure 2. Thus, Japanese imports have not increased, despite the strong yen.

• *Yield much better performance than other financial instruments available in the real world.* In all but two months over the past nine years, the FX market has fluctuated more than 1 percent per month, or 55 percent per year for a consistent winner in the FX market. Quite often, opportunities appear to make more than 6 percent per month. Similar high yield opportunities may exist in real estate, stocks, gold and, in the case of Japan, golf club memberships. However, such capital gains are usually taxed to effectively halve the yield, while the FX market is unlimited and unregulated in size, frequency of exchange, gains/losses and taxes.

What this means is that the FX market has become one of the largest investment instruments in itself, and is interchangeable with other instruments. At the root of this problem is the worldwide super-liquidity problem. In Japan alone, some $1.1 billion is generated daily from the private and corporate sectors to be invested. Since there are not many opportunities to substantively absorb such an amount of money in real consumption, the excess money ends up in the available instruments, or "buckets." For institutional investors, it does not make any difference in which bucket the money is put, so long as they are interchangeable and tradable.

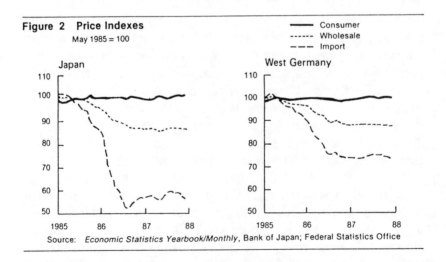

Figure 2   Price Indexes
May 1985 = 100

——— Consumer
- - - - - Wholesale
— — Import

Japan

West Germany

Source: *Economic Statistics Yearbook/Monthly*, Bank of Japan; Federal Statistics Office

Tokyo's stock market has already absorbed as much water (i.e., money) as any logical mind can imagine, at a PER of 80. The real estate bucket also has been filled, as real estate prices in central Tokyo have risen three to five times in the last three years. It does not mean that the utility of real estate has grown threefold. It simply means that it has absorbed as much money as it can. The payback period of an average office building is now over 100 years. Such a phenomenon can be understood only with the expectation of continuing appreciation in selected real estate properties. The $2 million membership fee for the Kasumigaseki Country Club is also reconcilable only when one discovers that these golf club memberships are *traded* in Tokyo. Even in Japan, the price of untradable properties, such as real estate in remote and rural locations, is going down, indicating that tradability is the key prerequisite for qualifying as a bucket for cash overflow.

Challenge to the Traditional Understanding of Economics

This new phenomenon suggests that several major changes are taking place, which would challenge the traditional understanding of economics.

(1) The traditional measure of inflation, the use of consumer and wholesale price indices (CPI and WPI), is obsolete. Until recently, overliquidity resulted in inflation, as a result of excess money buying up inventory in expectation of higher prices. Today, in an era of worldwide oversupply, excess money is contained in tradable buckets, and has not harmed the greater public by increasing inflation. This is because higher prices are certain to discourage demand. When supply is tightened, there is always a high probability of inflation. We are living with a zebra-like inflation today, where CPI and WPI are stable, while real estate and stock prices are sky high. In a way, the creation and discovery of these liquidity buckets, and the successful containment of excess money therein, have been the key ingredients in curbing inflation. Governments can take little of the credit for this success. Their sugar-coated monetary policies would have created unmanageable inflation across the board, were it not for the invention of the globally interlinked buckets and the occasional "leaky" buckets which act as "black holes" (Figure 3).

(2) The world's money supply has gone beyond the control of any single government. Through interlinkage and the active FX empire, money can now travel across national borders electronical-

Figure 3   The Buckets of Super Liquidity and Interchangeability

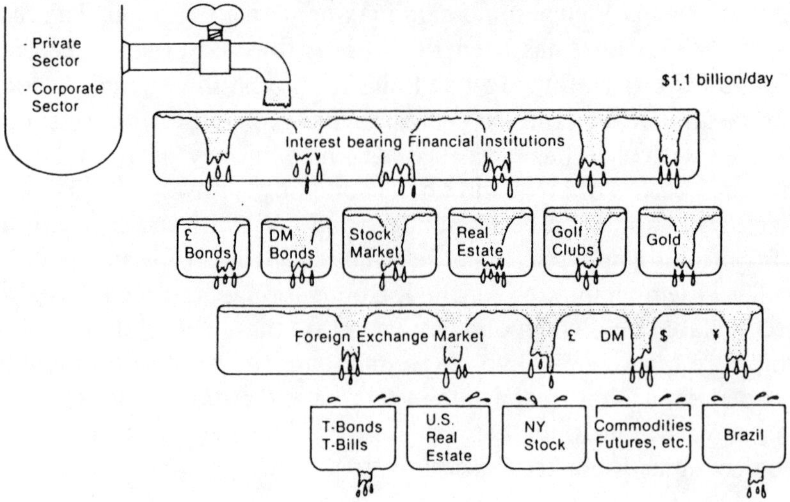

ly in milli seconds. Even if the BOJ tightens the money supply, a Japanese banker can borrow an impact loan instantaneously from abroad.

(3)   Monetary interlinkage has created dollar-based markets in Japan and yen-based markets elsewhere. In fact, the U.S. has created an opportunity to invite a $50 billion investment by the Japanese through its trade deficit with Japan. The dollar-based trade deficit is nothing but an accounts receivable for the U.S., as greenbacks must eventually be used to buy something American. They may make a detour via OPEC or Brazil, but U.S. trade payments are bound to come back to the U.S. In the long term, the trade balance must equal the capital-account balance, unless the country goes default or bankrupt.

(4)   The notion of interest has become obsolete. Such attractive profit-making opportunities as speculative buckets lure financial institutions to stay within the non-interest-bearing FX market, stocks and real estate, rather than seeking investment opportunities in the "real" world. Lately, the American government has persistently asked Japan and West Germany to lower interest rates in order to keep the large spread with the U.S. Recently, as the U.S. interest rate has gone up, the spread has widened to something like 6 percent *per year*. That is still far too small to attract money from Japan or West Germany, whose currencies have appreciated against the dollar by over 40 percent in a year. The FX empire's

profit-making opportunities on the exchange itself could reach over 50 percent per year, making any interest-bearing instruments look rather boring.

• *Be ineffective in correcting the trade imbalance.* Despite the currency adjustment of 40 percent to 50 percent, the U.S. trade deficit with Japan, and most countries in Europe, has not come down, at least in dollar terms. This suggests, on the one hand, that the use of the dollar to measure the imbalance is a futile effort when its value, relative to other currencies, is dwindling. It also suggests, on the other hand, that the exchange rate is a poor instrument by which to adjust the trade imbalance. Unlike the days of David Ricardo and Adam Smith, when internationally traded goods were primarily commodities, the leading exporters today are much more specialized in manufacturing. The impact of the labor rate and raw materials is far less important today than in the past.

Industries tend to cluster to gain competitiveness and flourish as a whole, as in the case of aerospace in the U.S., chemicals in West Germany, and cameras and consumer electronics in Japan. It takes decades to build up the infrastructure needed to excel in any industry worldwide. Once built, it again takes a long time to relocate. Currency rates are too temporary to affect corporate decisions to relocate. Currencies fluctuate. They seem to hit highs (or lows) every two years. Plants can't be moved around at this pace. As a result, higher prices may be passed on to the market, as in the case of German cars in the U.S., or costs may be reduced significantly so as not to pass on the full impact of the exchange rate fluctuation to the customer, as in the case of Japanese consumer electronics.

It is a lot easier to absorb the impact of FX rate fluctuations within the existing industrial cluster, or cascade of old vendors/subcontractors, rather than relocate the plant to, say, the U.S., and start with brand-new vendors and subcontractors who are at the starting (high) point of the learning curve. These clusters have more resilience against changes in FX than might be indicated by a straightforward comparison of wage rates under a new exchange rate. The Group of Five, here again, wrongly assumed that a correction in exchange rates would correct the problem of U.S. industrial competitiveness, and thereby rectify its huge trade imbalance.

• *Be extremely sensitive to macroeconomic results and government officials' announcements.* If FX were reflective of the fundamentals of the economy, then such extreme moves, creating

peaks and valleys, would not result. This is because economies —
that of Japan or, for that matter, of the U.S. — do not fluctuate so
vigorously, daily or monthly. As far as I can see from Tokyo, the
Japanese economy is changing only slowly and consistently, and I
believe the same is true with the American economy.

From a detailed analysis of the Reuter and the Telerate services
(information terminals which almost all traders worldwide rely on
today), it is clear that the daily and even weekly rates are severely
affected by American officials' public and implied statements.
Figure 4 is an example of such an analysis of exchange-rate change,
with indications of captions from the Telerate news as they appeared on the screen. Traders watch these screens not so much with
a great knowledge of the world economy, but with curiosity as to
how their fellow traders will interpret the same information.
Reading the mind of the traders is often more profitable than
knowing the fundamentals. It is thus the announcement of the fundamentals that drives the FX market, as opposed to the fundamentals themselves.

• *Change in a surge from one extreme to another.* For example,
the yen-dollar rate changed from a low of 259 in February of 1985
to a high of 137 in May of 1987, or almost 50 percent — far from
the notion of currency adjustment. Though drastic, this was not
the first time that the exchange rate had moved so significantly. In
fact, the history of the pound-dollar relationship before and during
the pre-Great Depression era is almost as 'wild' as the recent
dollar-yen relationship. In fact, one could conclude that the ex-

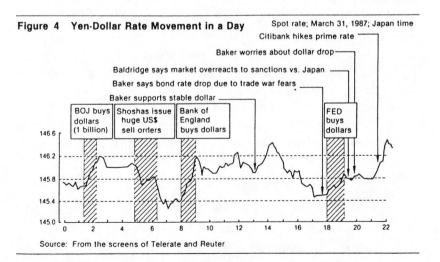

Figure 4   Yen-Dollar Rate Movement in a Day   Spot rate; March 31, 1987; Japan time

Source: From the screens of Telerate and Reuter

change rate does not hesitate at a certain level, but swings somewhat like a pendulum in about a two- to three-year cycle. The rate of change is particularly fast at the cycle's peak or bottom point.

The Political Paradigm

The two countries' fundamentals obviously do not switch position so dramatically in such a short term. What has changed 180 degrees during recent times is the American government's fundamental belief. Several years ago, the U.S. wanted to adopt a "strong dollar, strong America" policy known as Reaganomics. This policy has resulted in the twin deficits of the government budget and foreign trade. The U.S. recipe was to deal with the latter first by reversing its belief to that of weak dollars. The two countries' fundamentals have changed consistently over the decade at about 3 percent per annum, reflecting the differences in, e.g., productivity, rate of inflation and the interest rate. This suggests that the right exchange rate would have been ¥170-¥180 to the dollar at the end of 1987, or ¥160-¥170 at the end of 1989, instead of the current range of ¥140.

As we analyze the currency market, we need to incorporate this force at work, which can be described as the political paradigm. This paradigm is severely affected by American government officials, since they voice their beliefs, whatever they may be, more strongly and more aggressively than anybody else, particularly at turning points, or peaks and valleys. The Reuters of this world carry basically English information, and hence tend to overreflect the American, rather than the Japanese or the German, point of view, particularly in the minds of money traders.

The paradigm is the weighted psychology of the traders' reading as to which way the exchange rate goes. For example, a lot of Japanese money traders know that ¥140/$1 is too high and personally feel that the rate should bounce back. However, they also know that their fellow traders around the world hear much more about U.S. Treasury Secretary James Baker's point of view than that of our Finance Minister Kiichi Miyazawa.

People dealing with consumer-packaged goods are normally sensitive to the share of shelf space. They believe that if one can take up a larger area on the supermarket shelf for a given product, it can get a higher share of the market. A similar attitude prevails in the FX market. A higher share of the screen, particularly with the

Reuter News and Telerates, which over 90 percent of the currency traders around the world watch, tends to dominate the mind share of the traders, hence impacting substantially on the exchange rate.

Assumptions in the Currency Model

From these observations, we can construct a set of assumptions about the currency market. For the sake of simplicity and clarity, I will use the dollar-yen relationship and the Japan-U.S. economies as key drivers. This does not mean that such is the case in the real world. But I do believe that the simplified model is a useful first step in constructing a mathematical model to explain, and hopefully predict, the unusual behavior of the existing currency market. I have identified five fundamental forces at work which influence collectively, to come up with one number, i.e., the currency exchange rate:

1. Trading power for goods transfer
2. Financial fundamentals for capital transfer
3. Asset purchasing equilibrium
4. Political paradigms or commonly-held beliefs
5. Money traders' desire to make profits

The traditional fundamentals included such things as relative productivity gains and interest rates. I have tried to separate the factors affecting the competitiveness of the goods, such as productivity, from others which affect the flow of money in financial fundamentals, and have included them in trading power. In this fashion, we can more clearly understand the impact of the currency exchange rate on trade, and the flow of capital investment as a separate phenomenon. Let me explain each of these forces in more detail:

1. Trading Power for Goods Transfer

If, for example, the delivered cost of color TVs equilibrates between the U.S. and Japan at ¥140 to the dollar, automobiles at ¥180, scientific instruments at ¥200 and beef at ¥400, the exchange rate is set as the weighted average of equilibrium costs of aggregate tradable goods. Since not every tradable industry will try aggressively to export, however, some dominant products will act as standards for the rate setting. Automobiles from Japan, and lumber and wheat from the U.S., then, may overrepresent the process of exchange rate setting. Before Japan and the U.S. exchanged a lot of capital flow, this *relative trading power* was the dominant factor in setting the exchange rate. In the long term, the currency exchange rate is influenced predominantly by the relative competitiveness of manufactured goods.

However, productivity improvement is a function of the industry and capital intensity, and it is difficult to weight all industries. So, we have tested many relative indices to examine the long-term fit with the yen/dollar exchange rate, and found the wholesale price index to have the best correlation. If productivity gain is high, one can assume that the manufacturers do not have to pass the price increase to the end user, hence WPI may stay relatively flat. Figure 5 shows the correlation between the real currency exchange rate and the trading power adjusted for the relative change in WPI since 1973. We have pegged the latter at ¥265 to the dollar as 1973 was the year just before the energy crisis, when the two countries' trade was balanced, and also it corresponds to the period right beyond the initial adjustment phase after the float started.

This long-term trendline indicates that the trading-power-based exchange rate would still be around ¥180-¥200 at the beginning of 1987. According to this theory of relative trading power, the potential

Figure 5   Long-Term Exchange Rate and the Trading Power

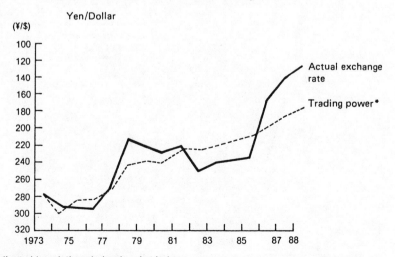

* Adjusted by relative wholesale price index:
  assuming trading power and exchange rate coincided in 1973 (Japan—U.S. trade was well-balanced and the floating rate system started in 1973)

for a certain exchange rate will have a reverse Gaussian distribution. Since the exchange rate is singularly set, any products which are not at the stable saddle point, or the bottom of this potential distribution, will be either too artificially competitive (left of center, as viewed from Japan) to export to the U.S., or too handicapped (right of center). For example, when automobiles became the dominant export item from Japan, textiles suffered, but chips had a lot of breathing room. Japanese chip producers did not take this margin as a heaven sent profit, but instead used it to reduce their prices in the U.S., only to be accused of dumping. The dots on Figure 6 are illustrative of the right exchange rate for a given product in exporting to the U.S. from Japan. The white circles schematically indicate the right rate for U.S. exports to Japan.

2. Financial Fundamentals for Capital Transfer

A second strong factor affecting the exchange rate is the *financial fundamentals*. Fundamentals usually drive *money* in one direction or another, as opposed to the trading power driving *goods* across national borders. The exchange rate, according to the financial fundamentals, is set primarily so as to equalize the return on investment. As such, it is influenced by relative differences in interest rates, inflation rates and the risks of investment. It acts as a

Figure 6. Potential Curve for Exchange Rate — Trading Power

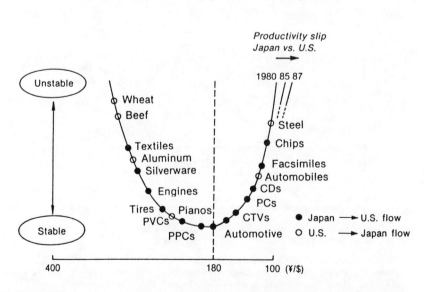

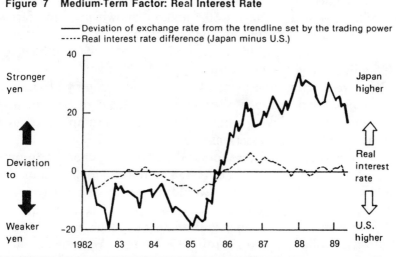

Figure 7   Medium-Term Factor: Real Interest Rate

two- to three-year, or midterm, counterpoint to the longer-term trendline set by the trading power. As shown in Figure 7, the difference in the real (i.e., inflation-adjusted) interest rate gives a pretty good correlation with the deviation from the exchange rate predicted by the long-term trading power shown in Figure 5. Over the past 10 years, the period with a higher real interest rate in Japan has resulted in higher yen than the trendline, and vice versa. The only exception has been the most recent period, when even the 6 percent interest spread has not produced stronger dollars. This unusual period is due to the effect of the political paradigm described below. It is expected, therefore, that with the removal of such political and pyschological pressures, the currency adjusts itself to a more normal trendline.

3. Asset Purchasing Equilibrium

An asset-based economy is a bubble. When you say that the Tokyo Stock Exchange is a 4 trillion dollar market, it is calculated on the assumption that all the stocks are valued at the latest price. However, if everyone rushed to the market and tried to cash in, it would crash, and the entire market would be worth a lot less than 4 trillion, perhaps a third of it.

Real estate has the same characteristics as the stock market. However, the asset-based economy, sustained over a period of time, has a funny way of becoming a real economy.

You can borrow against your assets as collateral. For example, if your apartment house in Tokyo has appreciated from $1 million to $5 million, your debt may be $0.5 million, allowing you to borrow up to 80 percent of the market, or $3.6 million. Using this capacity, you can build a mountain house for $1 million, buy a sailboat for $0.5 million, and travel luxuriously for $0.1 million.

You are creating real demand, or the real economy. These are not bubbles. So, bubbles can create real economy. Japan and Taiwan are now enjoying a burst of domestic consumption created by the bubbles of the asset-based economy.

Furthermore, if you were to use the borrowing capacity to purchase a house in Newport, California, and a condominium on the Gold Coast of Australia, you would be buying assets across national borders, using your asset base in Japan. If you have an idle warehouse in Tokyo producing absolutely no value, you could put it down as collateral and borrow $100 million. With this money, you could buy an office building in Los Angeles or in Manhattan, producing an annual return of 7-8 percent. This makes sense because the dead asset is now producing a healthy return, and even if Tokyo's real estate market collapsed, the U.S. assets would be intact. So, even if the Japanese bank wanted the lending margin to be adjusted, the U.S. asset could then be collateralized to generate cash to meet the Japanese bank's margin call.

It costs approximately $50 million to develop a golf course in Japan. Recently, a very nice golf course along the Thames near London came up for sale, at £7 million. This looks like a bargain in the eyes of many Japanese developers. While currencies are adjusted to equalize the competitiveness of tradeable goods, they are not reflecting the relative productivity and value of assets, which are often all "tradeable" across national borders through the mechanisms described above. In fact, the more central bankers react to the statistical trade imbalance and try to adjust the currency accordingly, the greater the gap becomes for the fair conversion of assets. Cheaper dollars to make American goods competitive also make American assets cheaper, and the assets are unfairly traded.

Most macro-economists, scholars and politicians have neglected this asset tradeability, and made the assets a real bargain. The currency exchange rate should be determined to reflect the relative importance of all three tradeable commodities: goods, financial instruments and assets.

This is a natural consequence of a borderless world and financial deregulation. If the latter two factors were incorporated, the dollar could be a lot stronger than it has been recently, and the Japanese wouldn't have been able to convert their domestic "bubbly" asset-based economy into the purchase of precious American assets.

4. Political Paradigms or Commonly-Held Beliefs?

The paradigm in currency markets is like the Delphi method of predicting the future which no one knows for sure. For example, by asking a large enough number of well-informed persons, you would bet that, for example, a material that would exhibit super-conductivity at room temperature will be discovered by 1992.

So, even if Professor Lester Thurow is completely off base, if a large enough number of influential persons like him say that the right exchange rate should be ¥100 yen/dollar and that it would move down to ¥80 in two years' time, then the paradigm valley gets deeper, and people start actually betting on it. As more and more people buy the yen to enjoy the appreciation, it will actually happen that the yen will climb up to ¥100 to the dollar.

On the other hand, a brave man with great credibility might say "No, the right rate is actually ¥200, since the Japanese economy is destroyed, and after all, the U.S. economy is much stronger than people thought." At that point, when the major upward move stops, and the rate of exchange-rate change becomes smaller than the interest spread between the two countries, investing in the dollar would become more attractive. As people move in the other direction, they start making exchange gains as well as interest gains. It becomes much more profitable to be buying dollars *and* investing them in higher interest-bearing instruments; the U.S. economy begins to enjoy an influx of capital and investments. Now most people would say, "after all, the right exchange rate is ¥200," which becomes the new paradigm.

In the real world, however, the scholars and the Kaufmans have seldom influenced the critical turning points. As shown in Figure 8 (previous page), powerful, and exclusively American, politicians and high-ranking government officers have made the turns and accelerations. Thus, I have named this force "political paradigms." The paradigms have been the major reason why the actual exchange rate has deviated so erratically from the more stable exchange rate expected from three other fundamental forces at work: trading power, financial fundamentals, and asset equilibrium.

Ordinarily, the political paradigm is a rather weak force, or a shallow potential to represent its shaky foundation. When a politician says that the right exchange rate is ¥94 to the dollar, he is using

Figure 8.   Creation of Peaks and Valleys in Yen-Dollar Exchange Rate (1977–87)

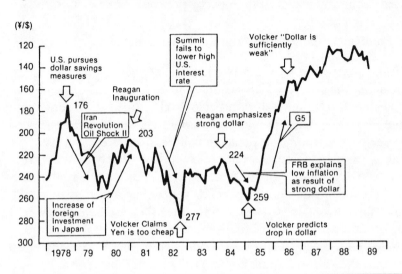

simple-minded linear thinking to generate the J-curve effect to balance Japan-U.S. trade. This is fundamentally wrong because the currency market has no such thing as the "right" exchange rate.

A paradigm does not have to be true. It only serves on aggregate to offer currency dealers fairly good opportunities to make money, and a comfortable feeling that where they are isn't too far off after all. The current paradigm seems to be around ¥140 to the dollar, as Messrs. Reagan and Baker have expressed their strong point of view that, "This is where it should be, and we don't want it (the dollar) to go down further." It was not so long back that the same government created a totally different kind of atmosphere, where "a strong America through a strong dollar" was the governing thought. It is also basically the same government (Bush/Baker) as in mid-1989, to now admit that a slightly stronger dollar is probably acceptable.

5. Money Traders' Desire to Make Profits

The *traders' desire* to make money may be endless. I originally thought that the currency traders needed to see the market fluctuate in order to make trading gains.

However, given the enormous short-term volatility, their needs are more than met through the daily, weekly and monthly hiccups which are not necessarily reflective of the longer-term needs to adjust economic fundamentals between the two countries in question. These fluctuations occur as the foreign exchange market's self-corrective action from the basic trendline, which is set as the compounded effect of the four more fundamental forces described earlier.

Figure 9 (next page) shows the monthly fluctuation relative to the average of the previous month. What this means is that, even during a period of general decline, there are opportunities within a month to clear a trader's position without a large loss and to take advantage of general trendlines. While the large surges based on the political paradigms have given money traders opportunities to make money, the peaks and valleys are not necessarily created by the traders. It would be safer to assume that the traders have had the "joy ride" with the paradigms, but they could be happy without the surges, so long as the short-term fluctuations yield 4-5 percent moves per month, or a 50 percent per annum for a constant winner.

Currency Exchange Model Using Potentials

Using the analogy of the non-equilibrium theory of physics, as in phase transformation, we have tried to synthesize the different forces at work to explain the change in the actual currency exchange rate.

At this stage, we assume that different forces form independent and different potential curves:

1. *Trading power* as the long-term and strongest potential;
2. *Financial fundamentals* as the medium-term, strong potential;
3. *Political paradigm* as the transient, weak potential, moving as a function of times, as the prevailing beliefs change.

As we have seen, the traders' money-making desires are more than met by daily, weekly and monthly fluctuations, and therefore we did not incorporate the fourth force in our model. A critical point to note is that these potentials suggest different optimal and stable exchange rates.

The result of our calculation shows that:

• A rather stable band of most likely yen/dollar exchange rate emerges as a result of the composite effect of trading power and financial fundamentals.

Figure 9.   Monthly Currency Exchange Rate Fluctuations 1977-86

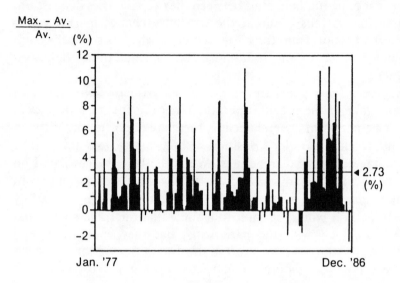

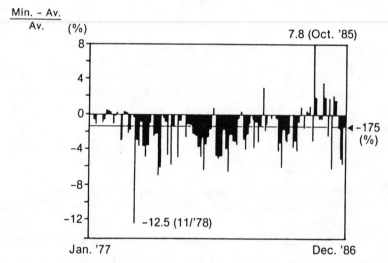

Max.:   Maximum of the month
Min.:   Minimum of the month
Av.:   Average of previous month

• When the third force, political paradigms, is added to this, we begin to see multiple-stable answers, or the saddles in the potential curve.

• Reflecting the hysterisis, i.e., multiple solutions depending on history, we come up with totally different solutions depending on where we start. A currency demands only one exchange rate at a given time. This means that while the rate may be set by the minutest factor in transition, people living in the real world must pay dearly for it.

• The exchange rate is affected by the change in paradigms, becoming ambivalent when the prevailing belief changes from ¥220/dollar to ¥140. However, the rate could quickly bounce back to the ¥155-¥187 range as soon as the paradigm swings back toward ¥220.

The probability distributions over time show a remarkable resemblance to the real life fluctuation of the currency. While the two principal forces create a rather stable band of rate change, the political paradigms can create extreme peaks and valleys that can deviate far from the stable zones.

In sum, we have been able to demonstrate that:

• Long-term rate correlates with trading power.

• Medium-term rate is affected by financial fundamentals.

• Paradigm, though possessing a weak potential, can swing the exchange rate when it is unsure and moved over time.

• Indeed, multiple answers are possible in the exchange rate as different and independent forces interact to determine a single rate.

• A probability distribution best correlates with the exchange rate fluctuations in real life.

• When the paradigm is removed, or changed, the rate can approach a more normal one set by the two principal forces.

Implications of the Potential Model

Admittedly, our model at this stage is to a large extent intuitive, although we have made our best effort to plug in available numbers. While we are still trying to develop more empirical and/or theoretical methods to come up with the shape of each potential, we believe this approach merits wide criticism and study, for unless our approach is fundamentally wrong, the implications we can draw from these simulations are quite significant:

• We have observed that the short-term profit-making opportunities in the FX market are much more attractive than any interest-bearing instruments. This means that the governments, trying to adjust the flow of goods and money through adjustment of interest rates, are outdated, or are not going to be effective, to say the least. However, as we have seen, the interest spread between the two countries can affect the medium-term flow of funds, and hence the exchange rate. However, when there is a strong political paradigm to push the dollar value down while at the same time trying to accomplish the influx of foreign money into the U.S., this is an infertile effort.

To make the interest-based policy effective, the political paradigms must be removed, or be realigned to be in concert with the direction of the two principal forces at work. Government should recognize that long-term competitiveness can result only through curbing inflation, as evidenced in WPI, which in turn is accomplished through real industrial productivity improvements. It should also recognize that in the medium term, i.e., two to three years, it can adjust the currency exchange rate by the interest rate. However, there is a certain limit to this ability, because the changes in the interest rate are going to affect the WPI and/or productivity gains. This is one of the reasons why the currency is non-linear. However, we have not fully developed the non-linear treatise in our model at this stage.

Back to Trading Power and Financial Fundamentals

• Policymakers and renowned scholars should be silent on where the "right" exchange rate is. This eliminates that impact of an unstable paradigm and allows the rate to be set by the two principal forces only: trading power and financial fundamentals. That sets a much stabler and slower movement, and removes unnecessary volatility in the market. Although speculative market participants may still want to enjoy profit-making opportunities, such needs are satisfied completely by the short-term fluctuations, amounting to 4 percent-5 percent per month. These "hiccups" will center around the fundamental trendline, and will not dare deviate from it too far. The money traders are basically cowardly people by virtue of the fact that it is a high-risk, zero-sum game. They can be likened to a scared swimmer whose toe must touch the bottom of the river bed. However, if experts and authorities say that he can go deeper and enjoy a faster flow without fear, he'd be tempted. The lack of such advice, on the other hand, will give him an enormous fright, and he, as well as his colleagues, will tend to swim back to the shoreline.

• A trade imbalance, *per se,* does not change the exchange rate. A bilateral trade imbalance is the result of the two countries' trading power. If Country A keeps buying goods from Country B, it will run out of money and stop. However, the money left in Country B must be used. If it is used to improve productivity and social infrastructure, then the trading power and fundamentals of Country B will improve, and then, and only then, will the exchange rate turn in B's favor. If, on the other hand, Country B could not find a use for the excess money and recycled it to Country A, then the net position is unchanged. In the long term, trade deficit must equal capital account.

The exchange rate changes as a result of trade imbalances, only because of the paradigm that higher (or lower) rates reduce the imbalance. Often in today's developed world, trade imbalance is the result of industrial specialization, rather than international competitiveness. So long as there is a commensurate recycling of money, it should not fundamentally affect the exchange rate *per se.*

• Government intervention in the market tends to make money traders more aggressive. When the BOJ or New York's Fed intervenes, it tends to create statistically more winners than losers in the market. The notion of a zero-sum game is the only built-in stabilizer in this already unstable market. It is the fear of losing that makes the market recover its sense of balance. If the government is ready to buy dollars when everyone wants to sell, it acts as a volunteer to lose. "Leave them alone and give them no hint" is the best way to make use of the two stronger forces, i.e., trading power and financial fundamentals.

Appendix B

NEW ZEALAND'S MAKEOVER OUTSHINES AUSTRALIA'S

by Peter Osborne

WELLINGTON—In a breathtakingly short time, New Zealand has become a nation transformed. The moribund and defeated society of 1984, the year that marked the beginning of a decade of great market reforms which started with the election of the Lange Labor government, has vanished.

One of the most protectionist economies has become one of the most open and productive. In short, New Zealanders are back in charge of their own destiny.

New Zealand began by following the path taken by Australia, where microeconomic reform and economic deregulation, with the float of the Australian dollar as the centerpiece, began in 1983. But if Australia provided the model and the trigger, New Zealand went much further and deeper.

Income tax had been halved. So has the price of a television set—an advantage of reducing protectionism. And deregulation has also made it possible for New Zealanders to tune in to more television channels.

Wellington has also done better than Canberra in tackling foreign debt, freeing the labor market and raising competitiveness through productivity.

Originally published in the *Japan Times*, December 23, 1944. Used with permission.

Since the advent of the Employment Contracts Act, New Zealand has experienced transformations in employer-employee attitudes and quantum leaps in labor productivity.

The ECA came into force in 1991. National awards ceased to exist and the protected position of unions was removed. All workers became employed under contracts either individual or collective.

Business confidence is now at its highest in 20 years.

New Zealanders have further to go than Australia before living standards return to the top 10 in world rankings, but they have faced their task well. Australia has not.

Both economies are coming out of prolonged recessions and are now romping along, with annual growth of around 6 percent. But Australia is heading for a hard landing, say many analysts, with a dose of reform fatigue. New Zealand, they argue, can reasonably expect growth, although somewhat less than 6 percent.

The difference is in the way New Zealand has focused on many of its economic fundamentals over 10 years.

In New Zealand, a government budget surplus has been achieved, which is likely to be 2 to 3 percent of gross domestic product this financial year, compared with Australian budget deficits of 3 percent.

Because of that surplus as well as a reformed Reserve Bank of exceptional credibility, a current account approaching balance and an industrial system that really does relate wage rises in productivity gains, the Kiwis are very much less likely than Australia to have to jeopardize their recovery with high interest rates.

In New Zealand, employment growth is the most obvious measure of labor market success. Employment is growing by 4 percent a year—its highest level in nearly seven years—compared to 3 percent in Australia.

Unemployment was 7.8 percent at the end of September—compared with Australia's 9.2 percent—and is expected to reach 6.4 percent by the end of next year.

As the runaway GDP growth of 6.1 percent fires up the economy, jobs and wages are increasing in nearly all of New Zealand's sectors. Although the booming manufacturing sector has produced nearly half of the new jobs, strong growth in employment also came out of agriculture, building and construction, wholesale and retail trade, and the business and financial sectors.

In today's New Zealand, industrial disputes are rare and localized and there is no equivalent to Australia's threatened wage breakout.

While Australia's current account deficit is likely to widen substantially and its net foreign debt position could blow out in the short term, New Zealand's current account deficit is around 1.4 percent of GDP, compared with Australia's 4.3 percent.

New Zealand's accumulated public debt, which remains unacceptably high, is bigger than Australia's, yet both countries' government outlays are around 39 percent of the economy. But a strong campaign by New Zealand to create corporations and, in many instances, privatize state-owned enterprises, is expected to improve the level of debt.

New Zealand's tax system has been cleaned up and the top marginal tax rate is now 33 percent, in line with the company tax rate. Unlike Australia, the Kiwis have already introduced a goods and services tax.

New Zealand also has its inflation more firmly under control than Australia. Since 1991, the Kiwis have held inflation to within the 1 percent to 2 percent range. Inflation was 1.3 percent last year.

In short, the economic recoveries of the two Tasman neighbors are fundamentally different.

New Zealand's is based entirely on improvements in competitiveness derived from improved productivity. Its inflation is low and steady and its budget going into surplus. There is no artificial stimulus. In contrast, Australia's inflation is rising and its budget is in substantial deficit.

It would be futile to argue that New Zealand's reforms have not been associated with pain. Most of the people experienced falls in their living standards and many workers lost their jobs as a result of the structural changes.

But the economic benefits flowing from the radical overhaul of the basic structures of the country's economy and public finances will continue for many years. In short, today's dizzying figures are sustainable. More so now that the New Zealand economy is undergoing rapid Asianization after decades of investment from mainly Anglo-Saxon countries.

Official figures reveal that Asians, who are especially active in tourism and property, are buying far more strongly into the economy than many traditional investors.

Already, New Zealand is fifth among Singapore's top investment destinations, with $1.5 billion invested cumulatively at the end of 1993.

Recent figures from the Overseas Investment Commission indicate that between them, Singapore and Hong Kong invested more than NZ $700 million ($447 million). Australia invested only 11 percent more in New Zealand in the last calendar year.

Add all the Asian money together, including Japan, Taiwan, Malaysia, and even Brunei, and the total comes to nearly NZ $1 billion ($640 million), almost 21 percent of total measured overseas investment.

Asian, and particularly Singaporean, buyers have taken considerable stakes in hotels and motels—around NZ $1.25 billion.

Almost 36 percent of New Zealand's exports now go to Asia, compared with 14 percent in 1970, led by dairy products, fruit, vegetables, seafood, meat products, computer software and legal, banking, and consulting services.

Appendix C

SINGAPORE SIBLING

Penang Narrows Gap in Race to Lure Technology Jobs

by Dan Biers

PENANG, Malaysia—History dealt much the same cards to Penang and Singapore, two tiny islands off the Malay peninsula. Both were colonized by the British and became thriving trade centers populated by industrious Chinese immigrants.

It was Singapore, strategically located at the top of the peninsula with a magnificent port, that long ago left Penang behind in the development stakes. With shrewd economic planning, the city-state became Southeast Asia's undisputed center of many sophisticated manufacturing and service industries.

Penang, though, is catching up. When it comes to new high-technology operations, more and more multinationals these days are heading for the Malaysian state, where operating costs are low compared with Singapore. Once known as the Pearl of the East, Penang now promotes itself as the Silicon Valley of the East.

"We're giving Singapore a run for its money," declares Boonler

Somchit, executive director of the Penang Skills Development Center, which offers people the technical training needed for working at the major multinationals.

Still, Singapore's economy remains by far the larger of the two—roughly 13 times the size of Penang's—with less than three times the population. And it remains attractive to investors; fixed-as-set investments in manufacturing hit a record S $3.9 billion (US $2.65 billion) last year and a further increase is expected this year.

The city-state also continues to be an important world manufacturing base for high-tech industries such as semiconductors, computers, and their peripherals. Last year, it accounted for 42% of the world's output of disk drives, and just two months ago U.S.-based International Business Machines Corp. announced it was setting up its first manufacturing plant on the island to make disk drives, which store information in computers.

But drive along the palm-lined waterfront of Penang Island's Bayan Lepas Free Trade Zone and you'll quickly pass a row of new or expanding factories that house some of the biggest names in the global computer disk-drive industry: Hewlett-Packard, Seagate, and Quantum. All told, there are 20 factories making disk drives and their components in Penang state, which also includes a chunk of the adjacent mainland.

A recent arrival is Komag USA (M) Sdn., which plans to spend more than 500 million ringgit (US $195 million) over four years on its Penang factory that opened in 1993 to make the disks for the drives.

Even after production began in Penang, says T. H. Tan, Komag's managing director, rival Singapore "sent missions here to find out why we didn't go [there] and if there were any second thoughts."

The Singaporeans "can see the synergy" developing among disk-drive factories in Penang, he says. "Once you commit to come to a place like this, you're going to be here for a long, long time."

Both Singapore and Penang were finalists for a new global service center for Quantum Corp., the big California-based disk drive manufacturer. "In the cost of doing business, Penang has the edge," says Lim Heng Jin, who manages the year-old facility.

Because both Singapore and Penang boast good infrastructure, government investment incentives, and support industries for high-tech companies, cost can be a deciding factor. For instance, the basic salary of a professional engineer in Singapore is equivalent to about US $36,000, or more than 80 percent higher than Penang levels, according to Hay Management Consultants (S) Pte. Ltd., which has offices in both Malaysia and Singapore.

Managing directors of multinational manufacturers in Penang also stress the high quality of local labor, saying workers generally speak at least some English and can be trained to operate the sophisticated machine that fills many factory floors.

Komag's Mr. Tan, a Penang native, quickly rattles off the names of several local high schools established during the colonial era that he says maintain a record of excellence. "They produce some of the top scholars of this island" and of the nation, he says, adding that many Komag employees come from those schools.

Strolling through his fast-expanding plant on a recent day, Timothy Harris, managing director of Penang Seagate Industries (M) Sdn. Bhd., points to workers operating sophisticated machinery that etches disk-drive heads with molecular precision. "If someone screws up," Mr. Harris says, "it can cost US $10,000."

Government and corporate officials alike in Penang publicly deny that the state's large ethnic Chinese population (Penang is the only Malaysian state that is predominantly Chinese) helps draw industry to the island.

But ethnic Chinese are found in almost all the managing director seats at major U.S. multinationals that aren't filled by expatriates. They also hold many of the other top management and engineering posts. "In some ways," confides a Western company executive, "they're more like Americans in that they live to work."

Indeed, Penang is considered to be so attractive by some corporate executives that a managing director of a U.S.-owned factory initially was reluctant to be interviewed about his company's decision to locate here, citing concern that his comments might help persuade competitors to follow.

While obviously pleased with Penang's booming industry, local government officials play down suggestions that they are in a cutthroat fight with Singapore for foreign investment in high-tech industries.

Koh Tsu Koon, Penang's chief minister, concedes there is "healthy competition" between the two locations in some sectors, but he says Penang views Singapore "not as a rival but as a partner in progress."

The Singapore Economic Development Board sounds the same theme, saying in a written response to questions about Penang: "We believe that the economic pie is large enough for everyone in the region." The board says its competitiveness isn't built on cost factors but depends largely on "economic and social intangibles including . . . national teamwork, manpower quality, creativity and international orientation."

Penang officials believe that Singapore's status as a sovereign nation also gives it an important competitive advantage. "Whatever they want to do, they do it faster," says B. J. Yeang, manager of the industrial and trade division of Penang Development Corp. And Singapore is indeed far ahead in such areas as developing tertiary education and technological training facilities.

Echoing others here, Ms. Yeang says Singapore is something of a "big brother," whose development strategies provide important lessons for Penang. For example, Penang looked at Singapore's Electronics Industries Training Center before creating the private industry-supported Penang Skills Development Center. Since 1989, the Penang facility has trained about 10,000 people in computers, programmable automation, and other areas.

"We have a lot to learn from Singapore," says Dr. Koh, the Penang chief minister, who regularly visits the city-state. "We'd like to learn their management system; they are highly efficient and effective."

Still, Penang itself gets most of the credit for its transformation from a sleepy backwater to industrial dynamo over the past 25 years. In 1969, a time of great ethnic unrest in Malaysia, unemployment was running at 16% in Penang and the local government was desperate to create jobs. An American-based consultant was commissioned to formulate a master plan and recommended creating an industrial base to help get the state's economy back on its feet.

Seeking labor-intensive, export-driven industries, Penang targeted electronics. In 1970, it set up its own electronics factory; two years later it created a free industrial zone to lure multinationals that were seeking offshore plants.

According to an anecdote told by Penang Development Corp. officials, when Hewlett-Packard Co. co-founder Bill Hewitt visited in 1972 to assess the island's potential, he was greatly impressed when a waitress whipped out a pocket calculator to total the bill for his dinner with government officials. Noting the ease with which she used the new gadget, he turned to the Penang chief minister and said, "Sir, if this is an indication of how the people of Penang would react to an electronics environment, then our decision is clear as to where we should invest."

Apocryphal or not, Hewlett-Packard was among the first of the electronics companies to set up operations in Penang. Multinationals in other fields also arrived, including Toray Industries Inc. of Japan, which began making textiles in 1972, and Mattel Inc., which has made toys such as Barbie dolls and Hot Wheels here since 1980.

Growth has been particularly brisk in recent years, with the number of factories in Penang's industrial parks and zones increasing by nearly 50 percent last year compared with 1989. Enquiries to the development authority in the first three quarters of 1994 more than doubled the amount from all of 1993. Unemployment fell to a meager 2.9 percent last year, and factory managers report they are scouring northern Malaysia for workers to operate the lines.

That success is creating some growth problems, most notably a tight labor market that has sent wages spiraling. Mattel stopped making labor-intensive Barbies in Penang this year, and many factories have had to automate further to stay competitive.

Dr. Koh, Penang's chief minister, now talks about entering a second stage of industrialization in which multinational companies in Penang would do research and development and be responsible for global sales and marketing of locally made products rather than just their manufacture. Intel Corp. is leading the way in setting up such integrated operations by having its Penang operations design future chips.

Here, too, Penang appears to be following Singapore, which offers incentives for multinationals to set up regional and operational headquarters that perform similar marketing and research functions.

Penang's local politicians talk about sustaining economic growth of 10 percent annually, which is about 1.5 percentage points above the current national pace. The state's per capita gross domestic product is about 15 percent higher than the national mark, but Dr. Koh says he doesn't see any political risks in developing faster than the rest of the Malay-dominated nation. "You cannot be lockstep for the whole country," he says, noting that neighboring states will benefit as labor-intensive factories move from the island in search of lower operating costs.

And no matter how much more success Penang has, Singapore will always be big brother. "We don't think we will reach a stage where we will catch up with them," says the development authority's Ms. Yeang. But, she adds, "we will narrow the gap."

NOTES

INTRODUCTION

1. Kenichi Ohmae, "Trade barriers," *New York Times,* April 17, 1983.
2. Kenichi Ohmae, "The mixed scorecard of Japanese management abroad: Backlash is mounting among companies that query how exportable are Japanese ways," *International Management,* July 1983.
3. Kenichi Ohmae, "Folly of U.S.–Japan trade imbalance, Part I: Outmoded statistics underestimate Japanese purchases of U.S. products," *Japan Economic Journal,* June 18, 1985.
4. Kenichi Ohmae, "Big 3: No longer solely American," *Detroit News,* April 21, 1985.
5. Kenichi Ohmae, "Deficit myths," *Wall Street Journal,* July 30, 1985.

CHAPTER 1. THE CARTOGRAPHIC ILLUSION

1. Kenichi Ohmae, "The real problem is that America doesn't know its own strength," *Japan Times,* June 2, 1987.
2. Kenichi Ohmae, "New study shows Japanese like 'American' goods made in Japan," *Japan Times,* January 13, 1987.
3. Kenichi Ohmae, "Interest ceases to interest with the rise of the FX Empire," *Japan Times,* June 16, 1987.
4. Kenichi Ohmae, "What moves exchange rates: New dynamics are challenging traditional theories," *Japan Times,* July 29, 1987.
5. Samuel Huntington, "The clash of civilizations?," *Foreign Affairs,* Summer 1993.
6. Kenichi Ohmae, "Japan feels 'powerless,'" *Newsweek,* April 13, 1987.

7. Kenichi Ohmae, "Japan still open to U.S. business," *Christian Science Monitor,* February 24, 1983.

8. Kenichi Ohmae, *Japan: Obstacles and Opportunities* (New York: John Wiley and Sons, 1983; Tokyo: President Inc., 1983).

9. Kenichi Ohmae, "Yokkakari: The cycle of dependence in the Japanese corporation," *Technology Review* (MIT), January 1975.

10. Kenichi Ohmae, "Japan's entrepreneurs," *Asian Wall Street Journal,* January 21–22, 1983.

11. Kenichi Ohmae, "Beyond the myths: Moving toward greater understanding in U.S.–Japan business relations," *Vital Speeches,* July 1, 1982.

12. Kenichi Ohmae, "Japan feels 'powerless,'" *Newsweek,* April 13, 1987.

13. Kenichi Ohmae, "Japan's trade failure: A trade imbalance does not equal a market-penetrations deficit, and in this regard American multinationals still hold the competitive edge," *Asian Wall Street Journal,* April 3–4, 1987.

14. Kenichi Ohmae, *Triad Power* (New York: Free Press, 1985).

15. Kenich Ohmae, "Interest ceases to interest with the rise of the FX empire," *Japan Times,* June 16, 1987.

16. Kenichi Ohmae, "Yokkakari: The cycle of dependence in the Japanese corporation," *Technology Review* (MIT), January 1975.

17. Kenichi Ohmae, "Special report: The myth and reality of the Japanese corporation," *Chief Executive,* Summer 1981.

18. Kenichi Ohmae, "A consortium may loosen up a stiff joint venture: Manager's journal," *Asian Wall Street Journal,* March 12, 1985.

19. Kenichi Ohmae, "Fact and Friction," *Japan Times,* May 1990.

20. Kenichi Ohmae, *Japan: Obstacles and Opportunities* (New York: John Wiley and Sons, 1983; Tokyo: President Inc., 1983).

21. Kenichi Ohmae, *Beyond National Borders* (Homewood, Ill.: Dow Jones Irwin, 1987; Tokyo and New York: Kodansha International, 1987, 1988).

22. Kenichi Ohmae, "The new rules of global competition: only "Triad insiders" will succeed," *New York Times,* September 2, 1984.

CHAPTER 2. THE LADDER OF DEVELOPMENT

1. Kenichi Ohmae, *The Mind of the Strategist: The Art of Japanese Business* (New York: McGraw-Hill, 1982; paperback, 1991; paperback, New York: Penguin Books, 1984).

2. James Fallows, "Japan's rice subsidies costly to them, and us," *Post Intelligencer,* May 31, 1987.

3. Kenichi Ohmae, "Dark clouds over Japan's economy," *New York Times,* July 29, 1987.

4. Kenichi Ohmae, "Unfair Trade?" *Business Tokyo,* January 1987.

CHAPTER 3. THE NEW "MELTING POT"

1. Kenichi Ohmae, *Triad Power* (New York: Free Press, 1985).
2. Kenichi Ohmae, *Beyond National Borders* (Homewood, Ill.: Dow Jones Irwin, 1987; Tokyo and New York: Kodansha International, 1987, 1988).
3. Kenichi Ohmae, *The Borderless World* (New York: HarperCollins, 1990).
4. Kenichi Ohmae, *Triad Power* (New York: Free Press, 1985).
5. Kenichi Ohmae, "Trade barriers," *New York Times,* April 17, 1983.
6. Kenichi Ohmae, "The fictitious Japan–U.S. imbalance," *Japan Echo,* November 2, 1986.
7. Kenichi Ohmae, "Japanese observer disputes U.S. view of trade war," *USA Today,* April 8, 1985.
8. Kenichi Ohmae, "Special economic report: Japan—The forces behind trade imbalance," *International Herald Tribune,* September 16, 1985.
9. Kenichi Ohmae, "Marketing: How to reach the Japanese consumer," *Financial Times,* March 9, 1983.

CHAPTER 4. THE CIVIL MINIMUM

1. Kenichi Ohmae, "U.S.–Japan trade tensions mask close private ties," *Asian Wall Street Journal,* November 3, 1983.
2. Kenichi Ohmae, "Deficit myths," *Wall Street Journal,* July 30, 1985.
3. James Fallows, "Japan's rice subsidies costly to them, and us," *Post Intelligencer,* May 31, 1987.
4. Kenichi Ohmae, "Folly of U.S.–Japan trade imbalance, Part II: Many U.S. firms find Japan a lucrative market, but they don't announce that openly," *Japan Economic Journal,* June 25, 1985.
5. Kenichi Ohmae, "A special report on Japan: Some foreign firms too busy making profit to complain," *International Herald Tribune,* March 19, 1986.
6. Kenichi Ohmae, "'Unfair' Trade?" *Business Tokyo,* January 1987.
7. Robert L. Bartley, *The Seven Fat Years—and How to Do It Again* (New York: Free Press, 1992).
8. Kenichi Ohmae, "Foreign goods made at home: It is popular to use Japan's $39 billion current-account surplus in the past year as "proof" that the Japanese market is closed to foreign goods," *Economist,* July 6, 1985.
9. Kenichi Ohmae, "New study shows Japanese like 'American' goods made in Japan," *Japan Times,* January 13, 1987.
10. Herbert A. Henzler, *Europreneurs: The Men Who are Shaping Europe.* (New York: Bantam Books, 1994).
11. "Marketing: How to reach the Japanese consumer," *Financial Times,* March 9, 1983.

CHAPTER 5. "NATIONAL INTEREST" AS A DECLINING INDUSTRY

1. Nathan Gardels, in the *Washington Post,* April 10, 1994.
2. Kenichi Ohmae, *The Borderless World* (New York: HarperCollins, 1990; paperback, 1991).
3. Kenichi Ohmae, "Deficit myths," *Wall Street Journal,* July 30, 1985.
4. Kenichi Ohmae, "Per favore confermere di avere ricevut bene," *L'Espresso,* May 27, 1987.
5. Kenichi Ohmae, "Japan's admiration for U.S. methods is an open book," *Wall Street Journal,* October 10, 1983.
6. "An interview with Ken Ohmae, international business management consultant," *Common Wealth* (China), May 1, 1985.
7. Kenichi Ohmae, "Rethinking global corporate strategy: The new global enterprise will be more deeply and strategically involved in fewer countries," *Asian Wall Street Journal,* May 1, 1985.
8. Peter Hartcher, in the *Australian Financial Review,* September 5, 1994.
9. Peter Hartcher, "Corporate Australia misses trade boat," *Australian Financial Review,* August 22, 1994.
10. McKinsey Global Institute, *Employment Performance* (Washington, D.C.: McKinsey Global Institute, 1994).
11. Michael Porter, *The Competitive Advantage of Nations* (New York: Free Press, 1990).
12. Annalee Saxenian, *Regional Advantage: Culture and Competition in Silicon Valley and Route 128* (Cambridge, Mass.: Harvard University Press, 1994).
13. Kenichi Ohmae, "What makes the Japanese so good in industry," *New Straits Times,* July 6, 1983.
14. Kenichi Ohmae, "Economy & business 'Fighting it out': Competition at home leads to success abroad," *Time,* August 1, 1983.
15. Kenichi Ohmae, "Malaysia can be in the world class: Expert," *Star,* July 6, 1983.
16. Kenichi Ohmae, "Foreign goods made at home: It is popular to use Japan's $39 billion current-account surplus in the past year as 'proof' that the Japanese market is closed to foreign goods," *Economist,* July 6, 1985.
17. Kenichi Ohmae, "Economy & business 'Fighting it out': Competition at home leads to success abroad," *Time,* August 1, 1983.
18. Kenichi Ohmae, "Japan still open to U.S. business," *Christian Science Monitor,* February 24, 1983.

CHAPTER 6. SCARING THE GLOBAL ECONOMY AWAY

1. Kenichi Ohmae, "Japan feels 'powerless,'" *Newsweek,* April 13, 1987.
2. Kenichi Ohmae, "Folly of U.S.–Japan trade imbalance, Part II: Many U.S.

firms find Japan a lucrative market, but they don't announce that openly," *Japan Economic Journal,* June 25, 1985.

CHAPTER 7. THE EMERGENCE OF REGION STATES

1. Kenichi Ohmae, "Forum: If they fall, so will our stock markets—Tokyo's soaring property prices," *New York Times,* October 11, 1987.
2. Kenichi Ohmae, "'Unfair' trade?" *Business Tokyo,* January 1987.
3. Kenich Ohmae, "Per favore confermere di avere ricevut bene," *L'Espresso,* May 27, 1987.
4. Annalee Saxenian, *Regional Advantage: Culture and Competition in Silicon Valley and Route 128,* (Cambridge, Mass.: Harvard University Press, 1994).
5. Kenichi Ohmae, A special report on Japan: Some foreign firms too busy making profit to complain," *International Herald Tribune,* March 19, 1986.
6. Kenichi Ohmae, "Special report: The myth and reality of the Japanese corporation," *Chief Executive,* Summer 1981.

CHAPTER 8. ZEBRA STRATEGY

1. Kenichi Ohmae, "Triad power: The coming shape of global competition," *Chief Financial Officer,* 1986.

CHAPTER 9. THE NATION STATE'S RESPONSE

1. Kenichi Ohmae, "Where the jobs are: Japan hangs out the 'help wanted' sign in American cities and eager workers sign up in droves," *Newsweek,* February 2, 1987.
2. Kenichi Ohmae, "Japan in Asia's new map: A dialogue with Dr. Mahathir Mohamad," *Shogakukan,* October 1994.
3. Kenichi Ohmae, "Who's really hollering about trade imbalance? Not 'nationality-neutral' consumers, not boundary-blind corporations," *Japan Times,* July 5, 1985.

EPILOGUE. A SWING OF THE PENDULUM

1. Kenichi Ohmae, "Forum: If they fall, so will our stock markets—Tokyo's soaring property prices," *New York Times,* October 11, 1987.

REFERENCES

BOOKS BY KENICHI OHMAE

B-1   *The Mind of the Strategist: The Art of Japanese Business.* New York: McGraw-Hill, 1982; paperback, 1991; paperback, New York: Penguin Books 1984.

B-2   *Triad Power.* New York: Free Press, 1985.

B-3   *Beyond National Borders.* Homewood, Ill.: Dow Jones Irwin, 1987; Tokyo and New York: Kodansha International, 1987, 1988.

B-4   *The Borderless World.* New York: HarperCollins, 1990.

B-5   *Japan: Obstacles and Opportunities.* New York: John Wiley & Sons, President Inc., 1983.

ARTICLES BY OR ABOUT KENICHI OHMAE

1   "Yokkakari: The cycle of dependence in the Japanese corporation." *Technology Review* (MIT), January 1975.

2   "Special report: The myth and reality of the Japanese corporation." *Chief Executive,* Summer 1981.

3   "Beyond the myths: Moving toward greater understanding in U.S.–Japan business relations." *Vital Speeches,* July 1, 1982.

4   "Japan's entrepreneurs." *Asian Wall Street Journal,* January 21–22, 1983.

5   "Japan still open to U.S. business." *Christian Science Monitor,* February 24, 1983.

6   "Marketing: How to reach the Japanese consumer." *Financial Times,* March 9, 1983.

7   "Trade barriers." *New York Times,* April 17, 1983.

189

8   "The mixed scorecard of Japanese management abroad: Backlash is mounting among companies that query how exportable are Japanese ways." *International Management,* July 1983.

9   "What makes the Japanese so good in industry." *New Straits Times,* July 6, 1983.

10   "Malaysia can be in the world class." *Star,* July 6, 1983.

11   "Economy & business 'fighting it out': Competition at home leads to success abroad." *Time,* August 1, 1983.

12   "A spark of militancy in the land of loyalty: Japan's once-docile unions start to fight back against automation and third world competition." *Business Week,* September 5, 1983.

13   "Japan's admiration for U.S. methods is an open book." *Wall Street Journal,* October 10, 1983.

14   "U.S.–Japan trade tensions mask close private ties." *Asian Wall Street Journal,* November 3, 1983.

15   "The new rules of global competition: Only 'Triad insiders' will succeed." *New York Times,* September 2, 1984.

16   "A consortium may loosen up a stiff joint venture: manager's journal." *Asian Wall Street Journal,* March 12, 1985.

17   "Japanese observer disputes U.S. view of trade war." *USA Today,* April 8, 1985.

18   "Big 3: No longer solely American." *Detroit News,* April 21, 1985.

19   "Rethinking global corporate strategy: The new global enterprise will be more deeply and strategically involved in fewer countries, choosing a few and getting to know their institutions and leaders well." *Asian Wall Street Journal,* May 1, 1985.

20   Interview with Kenichi Ohmae (unpublished; Chinese). May 1, 1985.

21   "Folly of U.S.–Japan trade imbalance, Part I: Outmoded statistics underestimate Japanese purchases of U.S. products." *Japan Economic Journal,* June 18, 1985.

22   "Folly of U.S.–Japan trade imbalance, Part II: Many U.S. firms find Japan a lucrative market, but they don't announce that openly." *Japan Economic Journal,* June 25, 1985.

23   "Who's really hollering about trade imbalance? Not 'nationality-neutral' consumers, not boundary-blind corporations." *Japan Times,* July 5, 1985.

24   "Foreign goods made at home: It is popular to use Japan's $39 billion current-account surplus in the past year as 'proof' that the Japanese market is closed to foreign goods." *Economist,* July 6, 1985.

25   "Deficit myths." *Wall Street Journal,* July 30, 1985.

26   "Special economic report: Japan—The forces behind trade imbalance." *International Herald Tribune,* September 16, 1985.

27   "Triad power: The coming shape of global competition." *Chief Financial Officer,* 1986.

28   "A special report on Japan: Some foreign firms too busy making profit to complain." *International Herald Tribune,* March 19, 1986.

29   "The fictitious Japan–U.S. imbalance." *Japan Echo,* November 2, 1986.

30   "'Unfair' trade?" *Business Tokyo,* January 1987.

31   "New study shows Japanese like 'American' goods made in Japan." *Japan Times,* January 13, 1987.

32   "Where the jobs are: Japan hangs out the 'help wanted' sign in American cities and eager workers sign up in droves." *Newsweek,* February 2, 1987.

33   "Japan's trade failure: A trade imbalance does not equal a market-penetrations deficit, and in this regard American multinationals still hold the competitive edge." *Asian Wall Street Journal,* April 3–4, 1987.

34   "Japan feels 'powerless.'" *Newsweek,* April 13, 1987.

35   "Per favore confermere di avere ricevut bene." *L'Espresso,* May 27, 1987.

36   "Japan's rice subsidies costly to them, and us" (by James Fallows). *Post Intelligencer,* May 31, 1987.

37   "The real problem is that America doesn't know its own strength." *Japan Times,* June 2, 1987.

38   "Interest ceases to interest with the rise of the FX empire." *Japan Times,* June 16, 1987.

39   "What moves exchange rates: New dynamics are challenging traditional theories." *Japan Times,* July 29, 1987.

40   "Dark clouds over Japan's economy." *New York Times,* July 29, 1987.

41   "Forum: If they fall, so will our stock markets—Tokyo's soaring property prices." *New York Times,* October 11, 1987.

42   "After the crash: Patching up a world of trouble—A Japanese view: Wise up, uncle Sam." *Washington Post,* November 1, 1987.

43   "Wise up, uncle Sam." *Japan Times,* November 8, 1987.

44   "Shaky foundation: Speculation kites Japan's reality boom." *Barron's,* November 9, 1987.

45   "Don't blame it on Tokyo." *New Perspectives Quarterly,* Fall 1987.

46   "Japan's management guru: Kenichi Ohmae sees through 'statistical deceptions' to offer an optimistic view of world trade" (by James Fallows). *Best of Business Quarterly,* February 1988.

47   "Quality of life lags for many Japanese." *Boston Sunday Globe,* February 28, 1988.

48   "Is Japanese savings rate really high? Conventional methods of calculation, which ignore differences between Japanese and U.S. customs, are meaningless when comparing the savings rates of the two countries." *Japan Economic Journal,* May 14, 1988.

49   "The world according to Ohmae: A noted Japanese analyst takes an unconventional look at the U.S. trade deficit." *The Atlantic,* June 1988.

50   "Americans and Japanese save about the same." *Wall Street Journal,* June 14, 1988.

51   "Low dollar means U.S. has become bargain basement." *Wall Street Journal,* November 30, 1988.

52   "Global economics: Multinationals shaping it, governments trying to figure it out." *Japan Times,* December 8, 1988.

53   "Global consumer vs. provincial government: Instant information makes it harder to fool people even some of the time." *Japan Times,* December 19, 1988.

54   "The U.S. and Japan: Partners in prosperity—Joint ventures for the 'Triad' market. *U.S. News and World Report,* January 1989.

55   "Why Japan could take a fall: Like us, they are mortgaging their future with reckless spending." *Washington Post,* January 15, 1989.

56   "Remove the fuse—but quietly please. Illusion of prosperity masks what's actually a powder keg." *Japan Times,* January 23, 1989.

57   "Don't worry, America: Money flows into the United States because it is an attractive market." *Newsweek,* January 30, 1989.

58   "The global logic of strategic alliances: Globalization makes alliances an essential tool for serving customers." *Harvard Business Review,* March 1989.

59   "No thanks to government: It's a delusion to think that Japan's current prosperity is due to Tokyo's guiding hand." *Newsweek,* March 6, 1989.

60   "Brave new world, Inc.: To superfirms, borders are just a nuisance." *Washington Post,* March 19, 1989.

61   "Managing in a borderless world: The global manager operates as an 'insider' in every market." *Harvard Business Review,* May–June, 1989.

62   "How to conquer markets: From the inside out." *Japan Times,* May 4, 1989.

63   "Immoral politics: The true scandal in Japan is not the recruit affair but a system that breeds grasping politicians." *Newsweek,* May 8, 1989.

64   "Economic detente needed between Japan and the U.S.: 'For better and for worse' Japan, U.S. are inextricably linked." *Japan Times,* September 13, 1989.

65   "Japanese fed up with adolescent politics—Asia." *Wall Street Journal,* October 25, 1989.

66   "Global village no place for Japan phobia." *Wall Street Journal,* November 29, 1989.

67   "Kenichi Ohmae speaks on world economy: 'Wealth is now created in the marketplace, not by the sun or the soil.'" *HBS Bulletin,* February 1990.

68   "Beyond friction to fact: the borderless economy." *Evening Sun,* March 22, 1990.

69   "Borderless economy calls for new politics." *Los Angeles Times,* March 26, 1990.

70   "Borderless economies: They spell the end of the nation state." *Daily Yomiuri,* March 26, 1990.

71   "Kansai: A fanfare of 'big projects.'" *Financial Times,* April 9, 1990.

72   "The benefits of competing with Japan: Japan has in effect a one-party sys-
      tem in which we now play the newly recognized role of opposition. Japan's
      own opposition parties have proven too weak to do this job on their own."
      Washington Post, April 25, 1990.

73   "Toward a global regionalism: We now see as much international as inter-
      national competition. North Carolina is not competing with Japan or Eu-
      rope but with Boston and Silicon." *Wall Street Journal,* April 27, 1990.

74   Kansai "How the mighty are fallen." *Economist,* April 28, 1990.

75   "Life in a borderless greenback empire. Never mind the trade deficit. The
      U.S. should remember: All dollars return home in time." *New York Times,*
      April 29, 1990.

76   "Japan's land prices: Some hope for a crash but worry about the avalanche."
      International Herald Tribune, May 4, 1990.

77   "Some analysts predict crash of Japan's 'crazy' land prices." *Washington
      Post,* May 5, 1990.

78   "Centralismo in crisi, fenomeno mondiale: Per il teorico della Triade il
      fenomeno 'Lega' non e solo italiano." *Il Sole—24 Ore,* June 28, 1990.

79   "Removing the curse of headquarters mentality." *Los Angeles Times,* July
      29, 1990.

80   "Japan and the U.S.: Rivals or partners? Ohmae has been arguing for years
      that the bashers on both sides are off base." *Washington Post,* July 29,
      1990.

81   Keynote Address "Global Competition in the 1990s." Australia's Foreign
      Debt, September 1990.

82   "Global escape from the HQ mentality." *Sunday Times,* September 16,
      1990.

83   "Burying the nation-state before it's dead." *Business Week,* September 17,
      1990.

84   "The interlinked economy." *Chief Executive,* October 1990.

85   "1990: Japan—Many are signed by stock, land crashes." *The Australian,*
      December 31, 1990.

86   "O livro do presidente: Nas maos de Collor, o mundo sem fronteiras de a
      receita do futuro." *Manchete Magazine,* 1991.

87   "China faces more problems than Hong Kong as 1997 nears." *South China
      Morning Post,* February 9, 1991.

88   "Kansai airport project criticized." *Japan Times,* March 1, 1991.

89   "Kansai area must channel resources to draw foreign investors, exec says."
      Japan Times, March 14, 1991.

90   "Recovery requires fundamental reconstruction: Recession will trigger po-
      litical reform." *The Nikkei Weekly,* April 11, 1991.

91   "Japan's bubble deflates." *International Economic Insights,* May–June 1991.

92   "The boundaries of business: The perils of protectionism." *Harvard Busi-
      ness Review,* July–August 1991.

93   "La mondialisation des enterprises ne fait que commencer." *L'Usine nouvelle*, July 1991.

94   "Retour a la strategie." *Les Echos*, July 2, 1991.

95   "Kenichi Ohmae: Bienvenue en utopia." *Le Nouvel Observateur*, July 25–31, 1991.

96   "Un Japonais bouscule la 'fourmillière' mondiale." *La Tribune de L'expansion*, July 26, 1991.

97   "Kenichi Ohmae: L'aube des consommateurs japonais." *Le Figaro*, July 6, 1991.

98   "Pacific partners: No country welcomes Japanese investment more than Malaysia. And the rewards have been sweet." Newsweek, August 5, 1991.

99   "The scandal behind Japan's financial scandals: The Japanese government has profited, directly and enormously, from the anomalies in the Japanese securities markets created by the securities firms and banks." *Wall Street Journal*, August 6, 1991.

100   Taiwan's full bright future. *Commercial Times*, September 2, 1991.

101   "'Singapore should go more regional and focus on services,' says Japanese expert." *Straits Times*, October 15, 1991.

102   Ohmae's "Regional State" proposal sparks lively debate—The borderless world is already taking shape, he asserts. *Business Times* (Singapore), October 15, 1991.

103   Information is fundamental force at work in the world: Dr. Kenichi Ohmae. *The Indonesia Times*, October 16, 1991.

104   Kenichi Ohmae: Diversifikasi Usaha Bukan Sekadar Persoalan Dana. *Kampas*, October 16, 1991.

105   Executive Lifestyle "Citizen Ken." *Business Times* (Singapore), October 26–27, 1991.

106   Kiat Bersaing di Era Globalisasi. *SWA Sembada*, November 1991.

107   "Regional state" urged for Kansai. *Japan Times*, November 21, 1991.

108   "Lies, damned lies, and statistics": Why the trade deficit doesn't matter in a borderless world. *Journal of Applied Corporate Finance*, Winter 1991.

109   Bush has a big job to do—at home. *Japan Times*, January 8, 1992.

110   Looking for an Enemy in Japan—The CEOs who accompanied Mr. Bush didn't include heads of companies that have been successful in Japan. Where were Coca-Cola, IBM, Procter & Gamble. *Wall Street Journal*, January 16, 1992.

111   Korean Companies aren't trying hard enough in penetrating the Japanese market. *Maeil Economic Daily*, January 23, 1992.

112   "Economic Borders Replacing National Borders." *Excellence*, March 1992.

113   Deeds, not words, says Japanese guru—Australia is accused of failing to take up opportunities because its attitude to Asia are "schizophrenic." *Business Review Weekly*, April 17, 1992.

114   "The emergence of regional states: The disappearance of borders." *Vital Speeches,* June 1, 1992.

115   Opinion. *Korean Economic Daily,* June 11, 1992.

116   (About Ken Ohmae's speech at KMA's 30th Anniversary.) *Korean Economic Daily,* June 11, 1992.

117   (About Ken Ohmae's speech at KMA's 30th Anniversary.) *Maeil Economic Daily*, June 12, 1992.

118   "Japan: Running against the status quo. Amid a global tide of discontent, Morihiro Hosokawa launches a political party with an antibureaucracy tilt." *Time,* June 22, 1992.

119   "Trens + Signale Japan: Der große Irrtum." *Manager Magazin,* July 1992.

120   "Beyond the wealth of nations: Unless the Beijing government develops the concept of a commonwealth of China, rather than trying to maintain central control over more than one billion people with one ideology, it will run into trouble." *Asian Wall Street Journal,* July 29, 1992.

121   "Japanese guru starts pressure group." *Financial Times,* November 20, 1992.

122   "Business guru to challenge Japanese rulers." *Australian Weekend Newspaper,* November 21, 1992.

123   "Ohmae sets up new political group aiming at fundamental reforms." *Asahi Evening News,* November 26, 1992.

124   "Business leader launches new political group." *Daily Yomiuri,* November 26, 1992.

125   "New group will support 50 candidates for diet." *Japan Times,* November 26, 1992.

126   "Japan: Draining the political swamp. As the ruling liberal democrats sink deeper into scandal, the search is on for new solutions." *Time,* November 30, 1992.

127   "Review & outlook: Democracy in ferment." *Wall Street Journal,* December 1, 1992.

128   "We won't be fooled again: The drastic surgery Japan needs is the kind that will restore transparency and freedom to a market that has long known only the intrusive hand of government control." *Asian Wall Street Journal,* January 11, 1993.

129   "Trade watchers should focus on regions, not nations." *Wall Street Journal,* January 27, 1993.

130   "Pied piper of Japanese politics?" *Business Times* (Singapore), February 24, 1993.

131   "Profile: Kenichi Ohmae, consultant turned politician in Japan. *Far Eastern Economic Review,* March 11, 1993.

132   "The Rise of the Region State." *Foreign Affairs,* Spring 1993.

133   "The ideal country: Activist puts citizens first in vision for reform." *Japan Times,* May 3, 1993.

134   "Call to end Japan's 'rice mafia.'" *Australian Financial Review,* May 3, 1993.

135   "U.S.–Japan trade fictions." *Wall Street Journal,* May 27, 1993.

136   "Canada Inc.: Kenichi Ohmae. 'I predict that as long as you have this 19th century nation-state model, it will be almost impossible to succeed.'" *Report on Business Magazine,* June 1993.

137   "Trade fictions create frictions." *Japan Times,* June 8, 1993.

138   "Our place in the sun: Australia cannot compete with Japan in building cars. But when it comes to building houses, we are light years ahead, and that means unlimited opportunities for Australia industry." *Herald Sun,* June 17, 1993.

139   "It's a clever country after all! How Australia can tap the Japanese goldmine." *Couriere Mail,* June 24, 1993.

140   "The vampire summit—Take Clinton's call for an international job 'summit'—What you see is a practiced smile for the cameras, but what you hear is just whistling past the graveyard." *Wall Street Journal,* July 7, 1993.

141   Interview. *Korean Economic Journal,* July 31, 1993.

142   "Death of the nation state: Studies of national competitiveness suggest that political boundaries make for economic units. This is an outmoded fallacy in an age where the region is king, says Kenichi Ohmae." *worldlink,* August 1993.

143   "Guangdong to go hi-tech." *South China Morning Post,* August 31, 1993.

144   "Getting a jump on 21st century: Unlike the damper being put on the rest of China, Kent Chen and Ray Heath report from Guangzhou that Guangdong province is racing ahead with plans for beyond 2000." *South China Morning Post,* September 2, 1993.

145   "Japan Inc. in need of long-time reform: The government cannot discuss serious policy matters for fear of losing control." *Financial Times,* September 20, 1993.

146   "How McKinsey does it: The world's most powerful consulting firm commands unrivaled respect—and prices—but is being buffeted by a host of new challenges" (by John Huey). *Fortune,* November 1, 1993.

147   "Plan ahead, Guangdong." *Asia, Inc.,* February 1994.

148   "Wirtschaft region. Ein Japaner rat der Schweiz: in die Apec statt in die EG." *Baesler Zeitung,* February 9, 1994.

149   "The Japanese economy needs surgery, not bandages." *Japan Times,* February 21, 1994.

150   "The end of a long winter: Japan's property bust batters the banks." *Newsweek,* March 7, 1994.

151   "U.S–Japan: Counting what counts." *Asian Wall Street Journal,* March 23, 1994.

152   "Malaysia needs a change in strategy." *Business Times,* June 23, 1994.

153   "Malaysia can be linked to emerging Asian giants." *New Straits Times,* June 23, 1994.

154   "To light a fire: Is Japanese society ready for a radical change of direction?" *Intersect,* July 1994.

155   "House that! Australia fumbles a $10 billion bonanzai." *Australian Financial Review,* August 22, 1994.

156   "New world order: The rise of the region state." *Wall Street Journal,* August 1994.

157   "Malaysia in the borderless world: Malaysian economy has changed to a value-added economy and has been very successful. In 10 years Malaysia has to think about in a global market." *Certified Management Digest,* August, 1994.

158   "Global Citizen Ken." *Economist,* October 22, 1994.

159   "No more trade negotiations: It is the time for politicians and bureaucrats to leave trade matters to the consumers and corporations." *Japan Times,* October 25, 1994.

160   "One-to-one selling touted as the answer: Mr. Ohmae urged operating the trading company to overcome the problem in Australia." *Australian Financial Review,* September 5, 1994.

161   "Nintendo Kid's Brave New Borderless World." *Japan Times,* November 16, 1994.

162   "Megacities seen as key to future trade: How Australia should be in the future?" *Weekend Australian,* November 19–20, 1994.

163   "Fact and Friction." *Japan Times,* May 1990.

164   "Japan in Asia's New Map: A Dialogue with Dr. Mahathir Mohamad." *Shogakukan,* October 1994.

FURTHER KENICHI OHMAE READING MATERIALS BY SUBJECT

Category of subjects/issue	*Reference number*
Trade imbalance	17, 21, 22, 25, 26, 29, 43, 49, 108, 151, 163, B-6
Trade negotiations	3, 5, 7, 23, 30, 45, 80, 135, 137, 159
Protectionism	92, 109
Insiderization/Global integration	6, 15, 19, 28, 60, 61, 62, B-3
Who are "they" and who are "we"?	18, 24, 31, 32, 52, 53, 110, B-2, 163
Interdependence	14, 56, B-4
Interlinked economies	41, 42, 64, 84, B-4
Currency and forex empire	38, 39, 51, 57, 75, B-4
Myths of Japanese companies	1, 2, B-1

ADDITIONAL READINGS

R-1   Annalee Saxenian. *Regional Advantage: Culture and Competition in Silicon Valley and Route 128.* Cambridge, Mass.: Harvard University Press, 1994.

R-2   Herbert A. Henzler. *Europreneurs—The Men Who Are Shaping Europe.* New York: Bantam Books, 1994.

R-3   Robert L. Bartley. *The Seven Fat Years—and How to Do It Again.* New York: Free Press, 1992.

R-4   McKinsey Global Institute. *Employment Performance.* Washington, D.C.: McKinsey Global Institute, 1994.

R-5   Michael Porter. *The Competitive Advantage of Nations.* New York: Free Press, 1990.

R-6   Peter Hartcher. In the *Australian Financial Review,* August 22, 1994.

R-7   Peter Hartcher. In the *Australian Financial Review,* September 5, 1994.

R-8   Samuel Huntington. "The Clash of Civilizations? *Foreign Affairs,* Summer 1993.

R-9   Nathan Gardels. *Washington Post,* April 10, 1994.

INDEX

About Kenichi Ohmae

Dr. Kenichi Ohmae is the Chairman of Reform of Heisei, a citizen's political movement, established on November 25, 1992. The Reform of Heisei movement now numbers over 35,000 members, and has as one of its chief goals the fundamental reform of the Japanese political and administrative systems. Dr. Ohmae is also founder and Managing Director of the Heisei Research Institute.

For a period of twenty-three years, Dr. Ohmae was a director of McKinsey & Company, Inc., the international management consulting firm. As a co-founder of its strategic management practice, he has served companies covering a wide spectrum of industries, including industrial and consumer electronics, financial institutions, telecommunications, office equipment, photographic equipment, industrial machinery, food, rubber, and chemicals. His area of expertise—and his special interest—is formulating creative strategies and developing the organizational concepts to implement them. Some of Japan's most famous and internationally successful companies continue to seek his help in shaping their competitive strategies. His counsel is also much in demand among Asian, European, and North American-based multinationals and governmental leaders.

Known as "Mr. Strategy" in his native Japan, Dr. Ohmae is regularly sought out as a public speaker. As an author he has published over fifty books, many of which are devoted to business and political analysis. He has also contributed numerous articles to major business and political reform publications (e.g., *Electronic Business, Wall Street Journal, Harvard Business Review*). *The Mind of the Strategist* (McGraw-Hill), *Triad Power* (Free Press), *Beyond National Borders* (Dow Jones Irwin), and *The Borderless World* (Harper Business) are among his best-known books translated into English.

Dr. Ohmae earned a B.S. from Waseda University, and an M.S. from Tokyo Institute of Technology. He then studied at the Massachusetts Institute of Technology, where he received a Ph.D. in nuclear engineering. Prior to joining McKinsey, he worked for Hitachi as a senior design engineer on Japan's prototype fast breeder reactor, the Monju. He now resides in Tokyo with his wife, Jeannette, and two sons, who share his spare-time interests in music, sailing, motorcycles, and scuba diving.